A PACT
WITH GOD

BE CAREFUL WHAT YOU ASK FOR

LORINE W. CALHOUN

Library of Congress Cataloging in Publication Data. All rights are reserved under the International and Pan-American Copyright Conventions.

atthetopoflife@aol.com author
starproductions5341@gmail.com author

atthetopproductions.com
greatestlifeforever.com

Vision Publishing

DEDICATION

To MY SON AND MY DAUGHTER, the most precious parts of my life:

MONICA CALHOUN, my daughter:

Monica, I am proud of you and the resilience you have shown throughout the years, and how you have shared it with others. As my only daughter, I watched you become a star in the incredible film, BEST MAN, and I couldn't be prouder of you. You have since starred in a host of other films and plays. You also write plays and produce and direct films. I am grateful that you have a son and live near me in Los Angeles. I am grateful to be your mother.

ERIC CALHOUN, my son:

Eric, I think you are the most wonderful son that was ever born blind, and one who wouldn't allow anyone to keep you from your dreams. It was my desire to make you independent, regardless of how people tried to take away that awesome self-reliance you always fought for, felt, and finally achieved with your brilliance and self-confidence. I dedicate this book to you and your ability to survive and thrive.

LORISE WILLIS MAYNARD, my twin:

Through your competitive nature, you set the bar almost too high for me to follow. I am the person you helped me to become. You are my mentor and my shining star. You are that necessary piece of my wholeness.

To the SATURDAY MORNING LITERARY WORKSHOP:

I am honored to have served as your president for more than ten years. Thank you for your dedicated support and the organization's contributions to our neighborhood, our schools, libraries, and children.

Further, I invite you to join me in dedicating my book, *A Pact With God*, to our awesome community and the world. I have nothing but respect for each of you, for walking this literary journey with me and the positive impact you have shared with me through your words, imagination, and creativity for a better world.

TABLE OF CONTENTS

The Beginning 1

Family Trial 10

A Mother's Dream 17

Deserter or Savior? 19

War 24

Momma –Ceo 31

Entertainment 36

Sex 40

Zenobia's Story 45

Louis' story 53

Education 60

High School Days 64

Higher Education 68

First Jobs 73

The Wedding 77

The Honeymoon 85

Till Death Do Us Part 88

Birth of First Child 95

Second Generation of Love and Hate 98

Leaving 105

Son in Crisis 111

The Move 118

Trip to Miami, Fla. and St. Thomas, Virgin Islands 121

Lorine W. Calhoun

CHAPTER 1
The Beginning

I watched time exploding into truth and understanding for centuries; then, one day, I returned to earth to learn the secret principles of the supernatural power that always Rescued Me. I am special because I made a pact with God. The force of it allowed me to be many years older in understanding and wisdom before being born. That should get me many advantages after my birth, I thought.

Lorine reclined on the chaise lounge by the pool wearing a yellow wide-brimmed straw hat. She always wore big hats that sort of became her brand. This one blocked the hot July sun from her caramel-colored face as she stared at the blue water in her swimming pool. At that moment, my mind went back to a time that I would never forget.

Before I was in my mother's womb, I supernaturally made a

1

pact with God. "God, if you allow me to go to Earth as a Black baby girl, I promise to make something of myself that you can be proud of."

God didn't audibly answer me, but soon after I asked Him, my mother became pregnant with me and my twin sister Lorise. He doubled what I had asked for.

The year was 1947, and we lived in the small southern town of Williston, South Carolina. I had looked amongst a lot of people on Earth and finally asked God for Ruth Eva Willis, a strong Black woman, to be our mother, even though she already had nine children. Now, why in the world did I go and ask God to give me that mother? Well, more than that, I chose Grover Cleveland Willis Sr. as my father. He was a short, Black man who worked in the fields ten hours a day to feed his family. My older sisters and brothers were young children running around the house and all over a dusty backyard.

My dad must have needed help working the fields, because what other reason would he have for creating all these children? Anyhow, under both good and bad circumstances, I promised to become a light on Earth, to do something that would please God and help other people in need including my family. That was my heart's desire, and I didn't even know how that would happen.

Against all odds and certainly against my wishes, I was given a twin sister, Lorise. Had I known anything about her, I would never have agreed to be her twin. No, not that one!

She was a kicker in the womb. She was a "taker" and rebellious too. Momma tried to keep the peace between us by rubbing her belly to calm Lorise down. She calmly talked about our sisters and brothers, especially that set of fraternal twins that were born before us; a boy, Ezekiel, and a girl, Zenobia. Momma talked about our father, too. Mostly, she said he was a devoutly religious man.

My sisters, brothers, and I looked at the ranking of our family like this: Momma and Poppa; then there were Mildred, 14; Cleveland, 13; John, 12; and Louis, 11. Then came the twins, Ezekiel and Zenobia, who were 10-years-old, the first set of twins before Lorise and me. Then Betty, 9; and Northa, 6; but it didn't end there. Finally, there was baby, Hubert, who was one-year-old.

I was happy to be the first egg fertilized. I could tell that sister of mine resented me and soaked up most of the nourishment from my mother's umbilical cord. Lorise would always push me out of my warm space. She kicked like a mule, but I was a little fighter in a quiet sort of way. I got in a few kicks and punches too; but she bullied her way to claim most of the placenta.

"That one on the left might not be allowing the one on the right to get enough nutrients," I heard the doctor say one day.

Now that was scary. However, in *The Bible*, Jacob and Esau fought in their mother's womb too. "You little scene-stealer," I screamed at my twin sister.

I could tell we were going to have trouble as we grew up. I just knew it. I understood what our elders were saying when they stood around talking to Momma while she rubbed her belly, saying that she should keep us both strong because the weaker twin gets mean, always having to fight to survive. That was the beginning of our competition.

A Pact With God

At 4:00 a.m., March 5, 1947, like every morning since I had been in that warm dark place that smelled like fresh peaches; I would hear the clanking of tin lunch pails. Poppa, my three sisters, and six brothers were packing chicken and bread sandwiches for their lunches. Soon, they boarded a truck that bumped over clods of dirt into the cool, dark dawn. Just before daylight, they made it to the cotton fields to make a living as share croppers. Momma would pray over their unseen moves. I would imagine their tired sleepy-looking faces, a long white cotton sack hanging around their necks, and how they must have felt when that sack was filled up with cotton, and they were dragging a hundred pounds of it in that 91-degree heat. I would cry for them in the womb. See, I already knew what a poor plight in life looked and felt like. I could see things outside the womb, as clear as daylight. I knew a lot.

Williston, South Carolina, had no nice homes, but the government gave each family in our tenement five acres of land. My family planted crops, and we owned a mule. Our water came from a well that was used by all the families. Poppa bought large blocks of ice to pack and chill the meat to keep it from spoiling. I always heard three noisy little neighbors running in the dusty streets. They also played in the small yards filled with collards greens and tomatoes. Where else were they going to play? One day I would be old enough to play with them, but the space wouldn't be any bigger, and I knew my family would need every inch of our land to plant enough vegetables to sell and to eat.

Besides all of that poverty, we had an outhouse. To keep from using it, I had planned to wear diapers as long as I could. That would keep me out of the little square-shaped shed called a "toilet." It had only one door, and inside was a wooden bucket that hung over a hole in the ground where the wind would shoot up your butt. No, thank you!

By the time Momma was eight months pregnant, she was always tossing and turning. Her constant shaking us up and down told me she was in a lot of pain. Her stomach was as big as a pregnant pig. Her feet and ankles swelled like watermelons. It was often said that the first twin in is the last twin out and that one would get all the inheritance. Well, the only inheritance I could hope for was to be the first one out of that tight space.

During my thinking, Momma said something that made me nervous.

"I'm having the babies now. Labor pain's coming every 30 minutes, and I'm here in this house by myself!"

I knew Poppa, my brothers, and sisters had already gone to the cotton fields hours ago. That's when round-faced, 34-year-old Sally-Lou from next door called out.

"Everything alright in there?"

Momma just lay on the daybed holding her stomach. "This pain's unbearable," she yelled. "Go get Nelly Now!"

Momma's best friend, Sally-Lou came over and we started toward the doctor's office that was about 50 miles away. I wondered how in the world she was going to get there in time to save us.

Even before Momma's conception, I had been given the gift of superior human insight. I was spiritually privileged to choose my mother and my father. I could see through the invisible screen of placenta to the unlimited power of the universe, and onto the forever heaven. I was chosen to guide us through this birth. I would have to spiritually get the midwife back home before my mother birthed us twins, or she would surely die. With my super power, I worked on Sally-Lou's thoughts for a mind change. Suddenly she turned from the direction of the doctor, 50 miles away and instead, headed towards town, about three-fourths of a mile away, to find the midwife We rushed in the midwife's house and shuffled her down the road. I stayed close to her to speed up her power to move faster than normal in that heat. The midwife started huffing and puffing and grabbing things to take with her. I moved in and spiritually wrapped my little arms around her neck and spurred her on.

"Come on, Nelly. Ruth is having them babies. Come on right now!"

We hit the road and I soared like an eagle just above the midwife. The old woman, wearing a long, flowered apron with many pockets, huffed and puffed some more. My vision followed her as she lifted her gray dress, swinging a bag of medical supplies.

Sally-Lou started yelling. "I told everybody that Ruth was havin' them twins this week. Told her last week to stop going to the fields ever' day. Did she listen? No. She's having them babies today and she ain't even due for two weeks.

"But you know Ruth. Always trying to feed all of them children and making more babies at the same time. Don't make a bit of sense!"

I injected Sally-Lou with a hard dose of spirit, and she kept up alongside Nelly, the midwife, stomping along in the burning heat.

Nelly wiped her forehead. "Sally-Lou, I'm goin' to run on ahead and get to work on Ruth. You try to get word to Grover in the fields. Sally-Lou darted into the corner grocery store and fed Ruth's predicament to the owner, Mr. Ben Stanley. He assured her he would take care of it. He always knew in which field Grover, Ruth's husband, was picking cotton.

At Ruth's house, the heat was as unbearable as an oven. Nelly, the midwife rushed in and set up a narrow make-do hospital bed by covering it with clean towels, and rags. She dragged in a tub of hot water as a gust of steam rose up. Her clothes stuck to her damp skin.

Meanwhile, Mr Stanley, the store owner had told Sally-Lou that Grover was working in the Stanford Farms field that day. She went there and the workers told her he was at the field just across the hill. Sally-Lou took off toward the second cotton field, wiping her face on the sleeve of her dingy white blouse. She heard a humming and stepped quickly off the road. It was old Mr. Barnes driving his truck.

"Get in if you want a ride," he offered.

Sally-Lou hopped in the back of the truck, her legs hanging over the side. Soon they approached Wagner's Farm and Sally-Lou spotted Grover working.

"Grover, Grover, come on! Ruth is having the babies," Sally-Lou yelled.

I smiled in the womb. I've never seen anything like my

daddy jumping in the air. He let out a yell, "Good God! Thank you!"

"Go, Poppa," I thought.

Poppa ran to the truck and hopped in the back. "Take me home, Sir!"

My brother, Ezekiel, took off toward the regular cotton field to take the news to my sisters. He was moving as fast as a streak of lightning and still made it home, not far behind Poppa. He pushed right past Poppa to Momma's bedside, "Momma, Momma," he said over and over.

Momma pushed her son out of the way, moving herself from place to place, groaning. The midwife turned her one-fourth of the way to her right side and stretched her legs. A loud, long, piercing, hell-filled sound burst out of her lungs. It hung in the air for a long time. The hollering took on an unstoppable sound of murder floating in the air and Lorise slid out of the womb into the bright new world, screaming. Momma went quiet. With no fanfare, I slid out a few minutes later.

Momma had her twin girls, born at 8:00 and 8:05 in the morning. I weighed three-and-one-half pounds. Momma and the rest of the world would never let me forget that I was five minutes late. Lorise had beat me to the punch. They didn't know it but I got tired of my twin sister and I used my special abilities to kick her out of the womb to see how it would feel to be there alone just for a few seconds"

Nelly spoke up, "Ah, name 'em Madeline and Merline."

Poppa shook his head. "Naught, Merline is a boy's name."

"Thank God someone thought of that," I smiled.

"Ok, this here is Lorise and this is Lorine. Lorine's got just one letter different," Momma said, moving the little blanket from my nose.

Momma, with her radar, said, "Lorise is the oldest, and the one with the roundest face."

That's right, I am Lorine, labeled the youngest for the rest of my life. I was stuck with that title, and I didn't like it one bit.

CHAPTER 2

Family Trial

No man can control heaven or hell, but courage is Divine and sets man apart from animals.

M omma had five children born in March: my brother, John D. Rockefeller Willis, March 4; twins Zenobia Willis and Ezekiel Willis, March 27; and now, my twin sister and I, born March 5. My birth must have added a heavy burden on our family because Momma had decided that we twins would be the last Willis children. Though I had been born just a month before, I understood that there was a lot of noise and needs in our house.

A few months of our birth, my sister Lorise and I were crying. We started to fight each other while Momma and Poppa fought to hold on to ten chickens, four pigs, two mules and two cows. That dirt farmer's wife, my Momma, with a sixth-grade education; and seeing no way out, walked into town the next week and went straight to Dr. Benjamin Walker's office.

"Dr. Walker, cut off this birth faucet, and I don't care how you do it." She demanded.

Now, if Poppa had known about her decision and action, he would have horse-whipped her. But she knew how to keep her mouth shut and to be fearless at the same time.

That's how it was with women who had first-hand teachings about lynching, children sold out of their parents' arms and Black people getting shot because a white man felt like it that day. All Black folks had to gather courage just to live day-by-day. If we felt far from God's power and needed to pray, we would pray.

"Let me tell you something," Momma said. "God will make you go through things to prepare you for storms that are yet to come." Momma knew that to be true because she had been pregnant for over 15 years straight when you included miscarriages and stillborn babies. Imagine not seeing your feet for 15 years! *What does all this stuff mean, God? Did you really mean to do that?*

Once I was back home, I instinctively knew. The fire was crackling under some soup without one piece of meat in it. That soup would be the only meal the family would have for dinner. But Lorise and I had a dinner of onions and garlic soup with cornbread mashed up in it and it tasted good. Having meat to eat in our household was a luxury, something that looked like one of those fancy dishes in *Home and Kitchen Magazine* that came in the mail. But in our house, meat was usually reserved for Sundays and holidays. That was no problem for Lorise and me.

By the time we were six-months-old, I was still as tiny as a newborn and Lorise looked normal. Momma added her two cents to my situation. "My doctor said Lorine lacks enough nourishment – mostly Vitamin D."

Sally-Lou said, "Ruth, you go and take that baby to

The doctor. I'll babysit Lorise and Hubert till you get back."

Sally-Lou was not only my mother's best friend; she was also the town's spiritualist. All the townsfolks knew she could see things – I mean, see things in the spirit world. So, when she announced that everything was going to be alright, everybody knew that there wouldn't be a lot of deaths for the next few years, and very few people would starve. It also meant that the Ku Klux Klan wouldn't burn down their houses. No one disagreed with what Sally-Lou said because what she said usually came true.

Momma surely wasn't going to argue with Sally-Lou, cause after her long hours of picking cotton, getting home after dark to feed the animals; and washing, cooking and cleaning the house, she was still connected to the Spirit.

Tears ran down Momma's face when Sally-Lou handed her the dimes and quarters she had taken from the church's collection plate – $1.25

"You take this here and pay that baby's doctor bill."

Momma got up with Poppa at 4:00 o'clock one morning and rode with old Mr. Barnes to the fields. Then, when everyone else was eating lunch, she put me on her hip, left the field and carried me to Dr Dan Samuels, our family doctor's office.

It was a dingy white room with thin curtains. After he examined me, he mumbled a few words.

"I don't know what's wrong with your child," and I don't know what to do to help her right now."

Tears welled in Momma's eyes as she left.

"I tell you something, baby Lorine; I'll never stop fighting for you as long as the good Lord gives me breath."

I wanted to say, "Momma, I love you so much," but at six months old, I couldn't talk, neither could I tell her I missed being in the warm womb, even if I did have to share it with that roommate of mine, Lorise. Momma kept mumbling to herself.

"I give Lorine Willis to you, God. If you make her well, I will always serve you," Momma prayed. I had been listening for her prayers for both Lorise and me. I could tell when it was a breakthrough prayer.

In the next three months, three more doctors gave me up for dead. We thought things couldn't get any worse, but after seven towns and eight more doctors, one doctor gave me a foul-tasting liquid that was as bitter as gall. It was so powerful that my bowels dropped out of my body with only one little piece of skin attached to my inside. After that, Momma started sighing all the time.

"You are so frail, baby Lorine." She stroked my forehead. "Please, God! Help her." This was now her prayer every day for two years.

Every day, my younger brother went to the fields with my oldest sister Mildred. She picked cotton and babysat him at the same time, something she had been doing most of her young life. She was picking cotton and always looked back to see how he was doing while she dragged him along on her cotton sack. We all called her "Momma Milda."

She would always say, "Pick the cotton youngins'. Pick the cotton. We got to make our quota of 100 pounds before quitting time." I think that was whatever time the day turned dark.

Poppa had his own issue. He would fuss, "Your Momma's got to stop going to all of them high-priced doctors."

Momma paid him no attention. She picked a few pounds of cotton, then took me to town to find another doctor she thought could help me. At home that night, she made it plain to Poppa,

"Grover, we got our children here. I'll not have another one die on me like John Thomas did, you hear? The sadness is too much for me!"

Momma had stood up for me and because of that, I gathered together all my love and poured it over her. I nuzzled my face in her neck.

One spring day, Momma took me to the next town of Columbia, South Carolina, to be checked by another doctor.

Dr Peter Lowery was a white man from Boston. He wore a crisp white jacket and had a kind smile. He lifted my diaper and jumped back.

"What the hell?" The doctor quickly composed himself.

"She's got rickets. Rickets is a disease of the bones, mostly found in children with a calcium, salt or vitamin D deficiency. It can cause softening of the bones." Then, with his soft, gloved hand, he gently pushed my wrinkled guts back inside of my skinny body.

"Here, give her this medicine twice a day, and she will be better," Dr. Peter Lowery said.

After three days, I wanted to laugh and crawl, because the gripping, slow pain in my stomach had stopped. Momma knew it was finally the right medicine because she said God had told her so.

This miracle took place because my beloved mother was strong, steadfast, and stuck to her faith. She didn't allow anyone or anything to make her give up. She kept going to doctors, even when the answer was always "no help here." With her by my side and her strength running through my veins, I started to think I could become the stronger twin.

Within three months, I was putting on weight and laughing. Momma was laughing and singing, too.

"Amazing grace! How sweet the sound-

That saved a wretch like me!

I –once was lost, but now am found;

Was blind, but now I see."

I began to cackle like a baby chicken instead of a young child. I began to take charge of my life; I had a future. I discovered that Lorise and I are mirror twins. What that means is; Lorise is a lefty and I am not. It wasn't always this way though; Lorise favored her left hand, but my oldest brother Cleveland stepped on my left thumb and this caused the fingernail to split. So, I didn't use it often. Zenobia, another twin in our family, became a lefty too. I wondered if something had happened to her right hand, or whether she was just born a lefty.

As time went by, a turning point came to my Momma's life too. Every day she talked about leaving the South. She took on a new strength and enough determination for all of us. She talked about getting out and taking her whole family with her to the Promised Land.

"Lord, what does the "Promised Land" look like?" What do people do there? Please tell me where Momma got those words, "Promised Land."

Lorine W. Calhoun

CHAPTER 3
A Mother's Dream

If we can touch heaven on the wings of God's love, dreams will come true by faith.

Momma, a dirt farmer's wife, owned those things that were God-given: free air, free water, and a natural ability to have children. One day in January in 1950, Momma looked around and realized that Williston, South Carolina's country farms didn't offer anything she wanted for her family, especially her children. No matter how hard my family worked, all of the income went for rent, food, and clothing. In addition to that, she remembered the fact that I nearly died because the family didn't have enough money for proper food and medicine. It might have been better to live a simpler life with firm family ties in Africa. When my ancestors were brought over from Africa, they were sold into slavery and ended up in what is now the state of South Carolina. Like most descendants of slaves, we even took our surname from the town where we lived. The "Willis Family" came directly from Williston, South Carolina.

My sister, Momma Milda, was now 15 years old and was in love. She wanted to follow her heart, and so was tired of all

17

the babysitting and cotton picking.

She dreamed of a life of her own, away from the constant responsibility of our family. She believed marriage was her ticket out to Philadelphia, the shiny "Promised Land" off in the distance, where a dream, a supposed paradise awaited her.

"You see, Momma," said Mildred, "there's no reason to live this way. In Philadelphia, I can work hard, get us a house and send for you and all my brothers and sisters. We will be just fine."

"No, Mildred, don't go," Momma pleaded.

"I have to go. Besides, I love him and you don't even have enough money to feed the other children. Poppa wanted a baseball team and he is happy. Now, I need some happiness."

"Poppa," Mildred continued, "chances for survival here are slim. I need to go to Philadelphia, where your brothers told us it has a better life than picking cotton. I'm going!"

CHAPTER 4

Deserter or Savior?

Faith cancels pain and only love can survive and make our needs lighter. At five years old, my family would talk to me like I was a little woman, and I listened.

So Mildred Dicks, my sister, got married at the early age of 15 to escape the responsibility of raising her four sisters and six brothers.

And, yes, she and her husband did make it to Philadelphia, Pennsylvania, and the promise still stood that she would look out for our family; and she did although not all at once because it happened in stages. Momma and most of the children eventually went. Poppa didn't go. Ezekiel had stayed behind. He had wanted to stay and to help Poppa on the farm.

It seemed to me that sometimes there were no "best" choices. Momma's biggest regret was that she was separated from her husband, and she always worried about him since he refused to leave the farm.

"Mildred had promised us a nice house in the white part of town, in North Philly, and she had kept her word. Now, you just come and live with your family," Momma told Poppa.

Still, Poppa refused to come North with us. He didn't like the city and gave up all hopes of making the adjustments. Soon after, we got a Western Union telegram that he had died.

I couldn't help but think it must have been from a broken heart. He had started building a new house for his family to come back home and live in, hoping they would return to South Carolina. But I heard the screaming and crying and someone was consoling the bereaved. "He died from sunstroke while laying the roof of that house."

Social Security didn't pay farmers in those days. So, he left us with no money and Momma was so broken-hearted.

But God provided food and gas money for us to drive back down South.

Before the trip back South, Momma sat us down and told us how it was down South. She read us all the rules:

"Going into the South and being stopped by police can be dangerous, and you can be killed. So, if the police demand your money, just give it to them, or you're going straight to jail. The Ku Klux Klan roams around at night, and usually, some Black person is beaten or hanged."

I listened with great fear as family members whispered about the things that happened to them in past visits to the South – "They stopped one of our two cars, but Louis gave the police his AAA credit card, and they took money off of it to pay for the ticket." The South for Blacks was a very dangerous place. Danger seemed to lurk everywhere around us.

The family rode back to South Carolina for my father's funeral. A line of dusty cotton-pickers marched up to the big white church. Poppa's casket was waiting up front for us. *When I marched by, I whispered, "Come back to Philadelphia with the family, Poppa."* I just looked at the body like everyone else without moving my lips. That was the last time I saw my father. That short, light-skinned man with straight hair and a smile that could kill, faded into the clouds, seemingly disappearing from me. A strong man, in love with Momma and the South. In my sadness, I sat in the first row of the church beside Momma.

Much of the heavy sadness lifted and left us as our family made such a fuss over Lorise and me. Aunt Katella and Aunt Hermine, my father's younger sisters, fought for their own time with Lorise and me. Following the service there were fried chicken, greens, cornbread, and pound cake spread over a long wooden table in the outer church. Like good Godparents, those aunts enjoyed fussing over us, picking the prettier child as "their" own twin. I doubt very seriously if they could tell us apart, but they loved fighting over us. That was the only good thing about the trip, the aunts fighting over us, "This twin is mine. No, she's mine."

Momma prayed, "Dear God, I now face the task of raising eleven children by myself. Let me never give up or separate any member of my family. Now I am a mother, father, and a full support system for eleven children. I will scrub floors and wash clothes in white folk's homes to keep my family alive and together."

Before I knew it, the family was returning to Philly to the white neighborhood. As the car rolled along, I went to sleep. It must have been a few hours later when I woke up thinking that I wanted Momma to go with Poppa's brother,

A Pact With God

Uncle William Willis. He was

handsome, kind, and never married. I thought it could be like in the Bible and Africa, where if one brother dies and leaves a spouse behind, another brother steps in and takes care of the widowed wife and her children. That never happened, though. Yet, Uncle William was always close to our family.

When we turned to Philadelphia for help, Momma faced the alternative of welfare or owning her house. You see, in those days, welfare didn't allow you to own a home and receive welfare. So, my brothers and sisters got jobs to help pay the mortgage during their high school years. From paper boy to baggers, to grocery store clerks, my brothers had no time to think about college or to follow their dreams. Everything was sourced into helping the family survive. We had to work to keep our house. Cleveland, my oldest brother, was 6'3" and wanted to play baseball, but couldn't because he had to work. Ezekiel wanted a music career, and he missed out. He had been in a singing group called "The Freedom Travelers," but that didn't work out for him either. Northa tried night school, and it took him years to finish college. Eventually, he became a social worker/counselor. Betty Earl married at 15, just as my mother and my oldest sister Mildred had done. Mildred landed a job working in Linton's Restaurant for 20 years. She'd bring home left-overs, and we ate better than we ever did in South Carolina.

Our North Philadelphia home became a way station for Southern relatives that wanted to relocate to the big city. Word spread about this new "Promised Land – the Land of Opportunity." Upon arriving at our house, our cousins laughed and pointed out the rare features on the gas stove, running water, bathrooms, washing machines with ringers, radios, record players, refrigerators instead of iceboxes and coal-burning furnaces. Everything fancy and new compared to the dusty, broken-down offerings of a home for a share cropper in the South.

My father's brothers ended up settling in Chester, Pennsylvania, while my mother's siblings settled in New York City. Still, even as legend spread of the "new" life in the North, some remained in South Carolina, just trying to survive. They chose to search for their happiness in a South that had almost defeated the Willis family.

The relatives that relocated, placing roots in the North and fought the loneliness; found some degree of progress and prosperity, but the ones that returned to South Carolina seemed to stand still in time. But who is to say which ones were happier? The relatives that ran back to the perilous South to contend with the devil they knew, or my mother, who fought poverty, prejudice and for Civil Rights mostly all on her own, to try and make a life for her family in this new land? There was no guidebook for her journey. I saw my mother reaching into the dark, deep places of her soul, trying to hide the emptiness of her new life. I don't think she ever got past the loss of my father.

For one life, she had given up a chance at another.

I often listened like a little woman, and she seemed to appreciate me listening to her when no one else would. Too bad that I didn't have the right words to give back to her, to console her, but then, maybe it was best to just listen.

CHAPTER5
War

Even in stressful times, God sends angels that light the way beyond imagination. These angels plant seeds in the soul for a better future.

"Come," Joanie demanded. Lorise and I walked to her, two houses down 15th Street. "You just move into the neighborhood?" Joanie continued.

Frozen with fear, I didn't look up to see the face of the girl who was talking. I just shook my head.

"Let me see your face!"

I could feel someone coming close behind us. Both Lorise and I moved slowly. Everything was strange in this new city – a new house and new people too.

Joanie pinched me.

"You *are* a nigger. I never saw Black skin before."

"I am a Negro," I said with pride. This was way before James Brown, probably a distant relative, coined the phrase, "I'm Black and I'm proud," and before Muhammad Ali said,

24

Lorine W. Calhoun

"We are Black Americans."

That racism that had reared its ugly head falling smoothly from Joanie's lips hit me right in the stomach. Momma had protected us from the Klu Klux Klan in the South by keeping us out of the main town, but now, nothing could protect us from feeling afraid in our nice white neighborhood. We were encompassed by it, submerged in a sea of whiteness. But this was at the beginning, as we were only the third Negro family living on our street. Times were changing and soon the current landscape would look much different.

Children are supposed to be childlike, but now I had to put on armor to survive. Negroes, who came to the North, were introduced to a new kind of racism. In the North, doors that looked open were actually shut. And '*White Flight*,' instead of opening doors – "making room for us" as they said – closed us out of jobs, education and social equity when the white families fled to suburbia. Within a year, only three white families remained in our neighborhood. They had all left, escaping to their new paradise – a place without us, to leave us behind, feeling trapped amongst ourselves by this kind of racism that was new. What were we to do?

Momma changed, but not in a negative way. With Poppa's passing, she had new independence. No one told her what to do, except Momma Milda. Her youngest set of twins, Lorise and I, became the center of her universe. Momma made sure that every child went to church several times a week. With church came the need for church clothes. Momma took care of the clothes. With church clothes came the need for "proper" church grooming. Zenobia, our older sister, cared for the hair. She washed hair, straightened and then curled hair and conducted weekly baths – first Hubert, then the younger girls.

Betty, our older sister, was head of wardrobe and family dinners, cooking dinner at 4:00 a.m. every Sunday: sweet potato pies, pound cakes, fried chicken, mashed potatoes with gravy, self-raising overnight bread, greens, cornbread and potato salad. That's when relatives would stop by – Aunt Dina, cousins Blanche, Jean and Doris, daughters-in-law Nellie and Carol; and our neighbor, Mrs. Vinson. My brother, Northa, and his teenage friends sneaked rolls and fried chicken off the stove before dinner.

Unlike my other brothers and sisters, when Lorise and I were a little older, we refused to wear hand-me-downs. We insisted on our clothes being new. Good thing Momma enjoyed sewing outfits by hand. So, we became Momma's showpieces. We were told what to wear, how to behave, how to recite poetry, how to sing songs for visiting family members as well as how to speak in church. If Momma could find fabric in the bargain basements of some stores, she would set about sewing new dresses for us. With her skills using the sewing needle, she built us a reputation and we had to live up to it. The Willis Twins became something of a hot commodity. Besides, Momma was no slouch herself at dressing.

The attention and fawning over us eventually went to our heads just a bit, and soon Lorine and I started fighting over who would take up more of the spotlight. We each wanted the best dress and constantly bickered over who had sung the best last time, whose poem was more lovely, whose steps were more graceful, who was more polite to cousin whomever or aunt so-and-so. If you could name it, we could fight about it.

Finally, Momma grew weary of our fighting over the clothes and attention, so, one summer, we were invited to spend three weeks with Aunt Lizzy, my father's sister-in- law, who lived in Chester, Pennsylvania. It was a happy arrangement. Aunt Lizzy sewed and made many more new dresses for us. She liked the fact that twins are strange birds. When called, we'd answer for each other all the time. We'd finish each other's sentences and made up a language only we understood. Furthermore, whenever Aunt Lizzy would call one of us, both would answer. This made her laugh. Aunt Lizzy was great fun. She'd laugh and make more dresses.

The main reason people couldn't tell us apart was that we would answer, no matter which name they called. Brother John called us Lorries and Lorea, renaming us. He wanted everyone to call him Rocky because it was short for his middle name, Rockefeller. John thought Rocky sounded great for attracting girls. As for me and my twin, friends and schoolmates began to call us just "Twin." And soon, we lost our identity. Our names remained unused until we separated to attend Gillespie Jr. High School.

War broke out in the ghettos of North Philadelphia when Hubert, Lorise, and I transferred from Kenderton Elementary School to the all-white Thomas Mae Pierce Elementary School that was almost three and a half miles away. Joanie, the white girl I mentioned, was a bully, and our leader. She told us who, when and where to fight. Bloody bodies scrambled home at the first sound of police sirens.

Now in an all-white elementary school, we had to show the whites who was boss, but after being there for only a year, there were no more white children left in the school to fight.

Not in the girl's bathroom, the lunchroom, or in the schoolyard. The very last of the few white people had moved to the suburbs of Philadelphia. The last few holdouts had now flown the coop, skittering away, swept up in the panic of integration. Well, so much for an all-white school. So, the Negroes began to fight each other. Because Lorise and I never ate much food, my mother complained that we were too thin to fight alone. We resolved that issue by double-teaming our challengers to win a fight.

Winning street wars, even with our "twin-attack" strategy, got Lorise's front teeth broken, and they had to be capped. Our opponent at that time, Chickie, who lived around the corner, was bigger and stronger than we were. God, I wished she had stayed around the corner. But as usual, someone would call another neighbor, and they would call another neighbor and on and on it went, passing a rumor that one of us talked about their mother. Then the fight was on with hitting, biting, spitting, and pulling hair.

Before summer came, there would always be a bloody battlefield on the streets. But when Joanie moved, our neighborhood went quiet. I wondered two things: were Joanie's parents fighting violently with each other at home? And, do bullies go to heaven?

In North Philadelphia, we lived near the railroad station. All the neighborhood kids played around the tracks at one time or another. Hubert, my baby brother, decided to ride his bike down the hill with me on the back. I fell off and knocked myself unconscious.

"I did it! I killed her," Hubert cried, tears starting to pour down his face.

I could see myself floating. *Hubert, stop crying, it's alright.* From my space outside my body, I could see the doctors in the hospital, too.

The doctor said, "She'll need stitches. Three needles and five stitches. She'll be fine."

Hubert said, "Oh, No! Now everyone can tell them apart."

I ended up with a scar above my left eye that would last the rest of my life. You can't keep identical twins entirely identical forever.

But we still looked enough alike that people couldn't tell us apart. Heads would turn when people saw us, double takes and questions always followed. "How does it feel being a twin? Do you have sex with your boyfriends together? Which one is smarter? Which one is prettier? Do you ever play tricks on people? Who is nicer? Which one of you is the mean twin?"

Before Joanie moved away, she lived quite close to us – walk outside our home, a left turn, and six houses down was where the bully lived. But a right turn and just two houses down was the home of Mr. and Mrs. George Washington. A venture to the left was paved with prejudice and hatred; and to the right were love and freedom. To get away from our house, we'd often go to Mr. and Mrs. Washington's porch. They served as mentors to my twin sister and me and planted dreams in our hearts that would last forever. They had been married for over 50 years and were loving people. Mr. and Mrs. Washington loved us and we loved them back. Since we were the babies of the family, all the love flowed down to us, we never really got to return all that family love, so it was wonderful to share that love with older people and to have them readily receive it.

Sitting on the porch together, we'd rock back and forth, creating a rhythm off our rocking chairs while singing. In the air of freedom and love – our dreams were developing – living in beautiful Los Angeles, Disneyland and attending UCLA.

We would appreciate the love of music as it seeped into Lorise and me from my older brothers and sisters and rocking with Mr. and Mrs. Washington.

We traveled the world in those four rocking chairs. We began to see a future in beautiful California and visualized living differently from all our other brothers and sisters. I had a vision of the Hollywood sign high on that hill.

I decided to live near Hollywood; Lorise wanted San Diego. When angels talk, we all should listen. To move far beyond the usual and expected and venture into the unknown was as exciting as it was overwhelming. Dreaming in a rocking chair, listening to older people who have seen more than you've ever seen and then marking goals to achieve the dream was the hope itself – the hope of a life beyond the ordinary, the hope of a life beyond the struggle. I would live in California and soak up its sunshine, movies, happiness and excitement. I might even be in the movies. Twins in the movies. Hollywood movies, where life was but a fantasy. That was the dream. But maybe …

CHAPTER 6
Momma – Ceo

One cannot totally control destiny, but one can control his or her thoughts, actions and love for others.

Sure, Lorise and I fought a lot, but don't most siblings? And there were times when we did have some good times together. We played hide-and-go-seek, stickball, soft-ball, and football.

Lorise was the best hiding partner you ever saw. I remember once it took me hours to find her. People think all twins have a special connection where we can magically hear each other's thoughts, but that never seemed to work with hide-and-go-seek. I was always stuck trying to figure out where she had thought of to hide next, but as with most children, the joy was simply in the hunt. I never got tired of our games. Lorise was my built-in forever playmate. I never needed to worry about loneliness.

Our home, a 60-year-old southern brick house on 15th Street, was a struggle for Momma to keep up. The two-story house had one bathroom and a walk-in closet on the second floor and a full basement that usually flooded every four years from rain or the water heater.

My brothers' room, the back bedroom, was the largest with two double beds, but it was also the coldest. The front bedroom belonged to the girls, decked out with three twin beds. Momma had the bedroom in the middle with a regular size bed and it was obviously the smallest of the three.

Hubert, John, Louis, Ezekiel and Cleveland slept in the mid-sized boys' room, but all five brothers did not sleep together; two had a night job so that only the other boys slept in these beds, at most, two together at a time. My last brother, Northa, lived with Momma Milda.

Lorise, Zenobia, Betty and I all slept in the same room. Momma put two twin beds together with blankets in between and in that crack is where the unlucky twin slept in discomfort. Betty was the older girl, so she got a twin bed of her own. With restless noises, restless sleep, feet flying into mouths and our weight pulling the beds apart, Zenobia, Lorise, and I fought for peace and covers. We maintained our dignity with laughter, tickling and pinching when we should have been sleeping.

Once, Momma placed a shoe rack with pockets over our bedroom door. Upon closer examination and to our surprise, Lorise and I found some candy in one of the pockets.

"Give me some," Lorise said, reaching for the bar in my hands.

We broke the chocolate in half and shared it. Lorise and I laughed, smiled and smacked.

"Momma will never know, right? I promise I won't tell

anyone."

We kept smacking on our chocolate candy that was safe in our mouths by then.

About three hours later, a gripping pain hit my stomach and after that, Lorise and I looked at each other and laughed. Both of us realized at the exact same time what we had eaten. It was not candy but Momma's favorite laxative, Ex-Lax. We spent the night and the next morning in the bathroom. That part was anything but funny.

Our old Philadelphia colonial house had backstairs. In Ben Franklin's day, the servants came into the house from their quarters through the alley, then through the backyard and through the back door. From there, they carried food up the stairs to their master's waiting arms.

Highly noticeable was the fact that people in those days were approximately only four to five feet tall, so the stair ceilings in the houses were built just high enough for a servant to get through. Building them higher would be a waste, I guess. Now, my brothers used those same backstairs. That was where they talked on the phone in privacy. We could hear them lying to girls about their love for them. We could tell who was on the phone and who was listening to their lies. Northa was the champ at saying sweet nothings and nasty things alike to girls and the girls seemed to go for every line. My twin and I built-up a kind of protective fence around us – men could not just talk a good game to us; they had to show us some real respect. A man needed to pull out our chair, let us wear his football jacket and make our mother like him.

Once, a gang-banger bit me on the cheek. I turned around

in a surprise move and bit him back. Then my brother schooled him. "You better not lay a hand on her." So, he backed off. We were all protected by the Willis Family Insurance Company – brothers one through six. Sometimes it was cool to have six older brothers.

We all watched our black and white television until bedtime. I was a walking *T.V. Guide*. Lorise and I knew what was playing at any time on every one of the three channels.

One particular night, we begged and pleaded with Momma to see "I Love Lucy."

She finally said yes and we huddled around the TV to watch our favorite show. At about nine o'clock, I heard my brother Louis' key turn in the door. Lorise, Hubert and I ran for our lives, tripping over each other to get upstairs. We then had to watch "I Love Lucy" from the top of the stairs; and then running back to the bedroom just in case Louis might look up toward the stairs.

With the absence of a father, Louis had taken on this roll of the daddy of the house; although neither he nor any of my older brothers quite matched my Poppa. Still, they tried on the "father of the house hat" at one stage or another. Daddy Louis was as hard as nails. He just had to look at us and we would straighten up. But, I have a secret on him. When Louis got married, he was hen-pecked. His wife treated him like trash. He obeyed her every command and there were many. Life is certainly strange.

Sometimes my mother was not in the best of health. She would cry out, "Oh, Lord have mercy," then she would moan all night, crying sometimes and praying sometimes. The meddling pain started at the age of 15 and lasted until she died. Doctors said it was arthritis. Neighbors made jokes that Momma's malady came from two brothers – Arthur and Ritis, meaning arthritis. They would say those odd names and laugh out loud. They thought it was a good joke amongst themselves, but it came at her expense.

What they never understood was that Momma had been picking cotton on her knees for 20 years. And she had kept going, even in bad health. No matter what, she was CEO (Chief Executive Officer), and Chairman of the Board of the Willis Family Fund. Whenever someone broke a rule, Momma had to tell each family member, gather opinions and decree a final decision.

Ruling with love and a robust stronghold was the secret Momma used to control the family and when it didn't work, she cried out with a howl. That made us feel less than human. A mother's love can be cruel, especially when she doesn't get her way. At the same time, a mother's love may be described as the bedrock of the family; we just can't do without it. Momma was a special kind.

CHAPTER 7
Entertainment

Most entertainment enlighten distract and refresh us – and often, it comes full circle to return what it has stolen.

What I have to tell you is not really about entertainment. You see, every society has its own set of superstitions. The Willis Family was no different; they had theirs from long ago. In the south, they believed that because John and Betty never left Momma's side, she was going to have twins when she got pregnant. It is also said that any pregnant woman knows that when a girl child stays by her side, she will be having a boy. The opposite is also true; that when a boy child stays at her side, she was going to have a girl. When two children of the opposite sex remain at your side, it's twins. I can prove that's true. It happened every time. Zenobia, a girl, and Ezekiel, a boy, were the first set of twins born into the Willis family on March 27, 1939. Now, there is the second superstition in our family and that is the significance of itching. If the right hand itches, it means good luck or money is coming. Left hand itching meant money would be needed or would be paid out. When your nose was itchy, a friend is coming to visit. Right eye twitching meant good luck is coming. Left eye twitching meant bad luck. It is as if your guardian angels just let you know what is going to happen in your life so you can prepare. Personally speaking, I discovered these things to be true; we have only to listen to our own bodies.

Then there is a thing in my family about names. Dad named most of my brothers after his brothers. We got smart and used nicknames. For example, Zenobia became No; Ezekiel became Z; Northa became Bubbles and Mildred is still called Momma Milda. Cleveland became Cleve and John D. became John. Then a nephew must have hated me because he named me Bean-Bug and named Lorise Beast-Bug. Of course, we countered and he became June-Bug, short for Cohen Dicks, Jr.

Here I was, thinking about all of that while waiting at the bus stop for four hours, talking all the time to myself in anticipation. My fifty-cent piece was burning in my hands. My destination was the Uptown Theatre, where another rock and roll show was about to take place. The lines extended over three long city blocks. You see, Motown had booked their major acts in Philadelphia at the Uptown Theatre. If an act could make it in Philadelphia in 1963, they could make it anywhere. That was the Motown Review.

The Miracles were on stage dancing, with smooth moves and mellow sounds. They moved to the rhythm with little speeches. I would scream and scream; holler, and holler. The louder I hollered, the more I enjoyed myself; I and about 1,000 other teens and their parents. For just fifty cents, you got in to see Moms Mabley, Smokey Robinson, the Supremes, Red Foxx, the Four Tops, Marvin Gaye, and other top acts of the times.

My brother, Ezekiel, tried his hand at music, but there was one problem. He sang Bee Bop on the corner. You know, one person starts a song, then the others join in. The sound does not turn into music, just love. Philadelphia became known for music and the 'Philly Sound.' However, the police didn't like teens singing on the corner. When they came around, you had to leave the corner, get beat down, or get arrested.

So, one Thanksgiving evening, the police arrested Ezekiel. They nailed him for being in a gang. He missed the turkey dinner with all the trimmings while family and friends enjoyed Thanksgiving. Well, Momma decided not to pick Ezekiel up from jail. That decision was a lesson for the rest of the family. Don't go to jail because Momma will never bail you out. Needless to say, no other Willis family member ever spent one day in jail.

Singing moved to the Willis family basement where 'The Freedom Travelers,' a gospel singing group was formed. Although the group broke up after five years, it did inspire my brother Hubert to try his hand at music. He wrote songs and encouraged girls to sing them. Hubert's girls worked at the Latin Casino and warmed up for The Temptations. The three or four groups he put together had stars in their eyes and left Hubert for greener pastures. Hubert made a living working with record companies and supplying talent.

My first celebrity crush was on Smokey Robinson. Claudette, the female singer in The Miracles, wore suits made of the same material as the male singers' suits. Over the years I struck up a relationship with her and we became friends. She invited me into her Beverly Hills home that was laid out with extravagant furniture and a view that smiled on us. We would even encounter the 'Beverly Hills Links.' That was the most prestigious Black social and charity organization in the country and I had never heard of them. Imagine that!

Claudette Robinson was hooked up to this organization and she invited me to allow Monica to be a part of paying tribute to her famous husband, Smokey Robinson! My first teenage crush! This is how entertainment came to me; taking God's road to success and listening to His guidance. Thus, Monica could be so influenced by the Robinson family for her career in the entertainment field.

I prayed for her protection and success; I hoped Monica would become a star. Do Black girls really become big stars without eternal damage to the soul, though? Some examples of Black stars are Dorothy Dandridge, Paula Kelly, Diahann Carroll, Vivica A. Fox, Jada Pinkett-Smith, Halle Berry, Angela Bassett, Nia Long, Lynn Whitfield, Nina Simone, Nancy Wilson, Josephine Baker and Jane Pittman to name a few. That connection could undoubtedly raise us out of poverty. I remained aware of my gift of being able to see things in the future. This stuff is happening in the future.

CHAPTER8
Sex

We die inside when hate and injustice create fear and lack of understanding.

Momma has radar, maternal wit, or a lot of ESP. She had a dream that told her that the house would be robbed when she was down south. She dreamed about fish every time someone in the family was pregnant. Her dreams were powerful and always came true.

My sister, Betty Earl, got married after Momma allowed her to attend camp. Needless; to say, no family member ever attended camp again. Betty married at 15, but her marriage didn't last. After three years, she came back home with a three-year-old child, John Thomas. Zenobia got pregnant at an early age, too. She had two boys without being married. So, Momma tightened the ropes on Lorise and me. Ruth Willis was on Mother-watch 24-hours a day. We could go to church and to school, but nowhere else. Dating was out of the picture. We got to go to the prom, but all our dates were double-dates, even if one twin didn't have a partner. I agreed to a first date with James. He was good-looking, but a real square. I decided to go to the prom with Gary. While Momma greeted him, I ran upstairs and put on the same dress as Lorise. I now had two dates, and Lorise had to pretend she was me. Neither of the boys was the wiser. Twenty-five years later, my niece, Rella, still hadn't forgiven me for tricking her cousin James. I felt bad about it. We didn't want to hurt anyone's feelings but at the time, it was fun.

Once, we dated two brothers, Ernest and Eugene. Ernest was tongue-tied and Eugene talked a hundred words a minute. We'd place the phone on the bed, go to the bathroom, and he would still be talking. Lorise didn't want to talk with him and neither did I. Then years later, Lorise named her son, Ernest Eugene Maynard, after our first real boyfriends. I'll never understand the reason why.

Most of my family members have some type of Extra Sensory Perception (ESP). I had premonitions as a child. I asked God to take that spiritual gift away from me. It scared me to dare ask God to do that and I wonder if I did the right thing, for no one could hide secrets in the Willis family. I would always find them out.

Another thing that scared me was sex. The doctor took one look at me and wondered what the hell was going on at home. Something was wrong with me. He looked steadily at Momma.

"Do you want him arrested?"

I wondered what he meant. "No," Momma said.

That was that. My mother had spoken. I knew exactly why she meant, "No," meaning don't arrest my oldest sister's husband, Cohen Dicks, Sr. He was darker than chocolate and worked in a gas station as a mechanic. His fingers were rough and big and smelled of gasoline. His eyes stared into my soul and he used candy to bargain his way into my body – to think

I trusted him. I had to look at that child molester every Sunday.

In 1955, I was 8-years-old, and little was expected of me. The knowledge of rape or incest was not known to Lorise or me. Teaching the birds and the bees to 8-year-olds was just not done. We didn't understand how to be afraid of people we trusted. I didn't understand that I should have been *afraid of him*. Things did not feel good when his finger pierced the inside of my legs. Why did he have to smoke in the room? I often wondered why the doctor asked Momma about arresting him. Something in my life was wrong, ugly, and shameful. My sister's husband had been molesting my twin sister and me. Lorise and I were so confused. "What happened at the doctor's office?" Lorise asked.

I told her everything, knowing that those eyes of my molester would follow me the rest of my life and the pain would reside in my soul as part of it. Now I think a victim can block out what actually happened and while I don't think brother Cohen completely raped me, Lorise had a different story. But what hurt me the most was that one dagger coming out of my mother's mouth, "No," meaning, don't arrest him.

We can cry a thousand times and still never quite understand what happened. So, I placed myself in my mother's shoes.

My oldest sister and her husband Cohen Dicks paid for the entire Willis family of twelve to leave South Carolina. Also, through their effort, we, the whole Willis family, were no longer getting $1.00 to $1.50 each a day for picking one hundred pounds of cotton in the South. In other words, we really didn't need it. My oldest sister and her husband had placed the family in a house in an all-white neighborhood in a nice area of North Philadelphia. If they locked up my brother-in-law, the entire Willis family's economic system would crash. My mother, Ruth Eva Willis, born December 26, 1926, would need to get money, clothes and food from another source. Maybe the other source would be worse or maybe not…

My oldest sister, Momma Milda's name, was on the deed for my mother's house. The little food and clothing Momma got from white people could never sustain our family. She needed Mildred and her husband's help. So, when the matriarch of the family said "no," it became law. Finally, Cohen Dicks did avoid being near us Willis girls. Maybe Momma spoke to him, but he was never arrested. You see, everything does come full circle.

Some 30 years later, my mother suffered from Alzheimer's. Her mind told her to finally address this man about sexually touching her girls. So, she attacked him verbally, with every fiber of her body shouting, "Cohen, you touched my girls. Why?" Her fingers pointed directly in his face.

Since the age of six, my mother and older sisters and brothers brainwashed Lorise and me against seeking a college education. "You are not smart enough. There isn't enough money. What possible good will it do?"

When we were studying, my mother would label the Library "The Bilberry." For those of you who don't know what the Bilberry is, it is the State Mental Hospital located just outside of Philadelphia.

These things affected me, and I acquired a negative attitude towards education. I felt if I could remain average or a little better, I would be in the safety zone. This attitude stayed with me from first grade through to the 12th grade. I had to learn the importance of an education the hard way.

Throughout my school years, the system threw me into segregated schools. I was honestly a victim of second-rate, predominantly Black schools, with uneducated teachers and inadequate school materials. To make the best of the situation in high school, I joined every extra-curricular activity Simon Gratz High School offered. My school days were happy and carefree. If there were drugs and gangs on campus, I didn't see any.

At eighteen, I graduated from high school and became aware that I lacked the basic skills to get a decent job. I read on an 11th-grade level, my grammar was weak and my math aptitude was not up to par. Self-improvement was my only hope. So, I enrolled in neighborhood tutoring programs and attended night school. At that time in my ill-prepared life and maybe my future, I began to doubt my mother, questioning her love and motives. Did she care so much about the family? Or did her background from slavery tie her to so much need and ignorance that she had to pass it on to her children? Well, I wasn't going to accept that gift of failure. I wouldn't! What happened next made me want to doubt the perfect mother I have described to you. Did Momma act for the good of the family, or was she just cruel? We all had our opinions.

Lorine W. Calhoun

CHAPTER 9

Zenobia's Story

We overcome obstacles through prayer and understanding.

My sister, Zenobia, one of the other twins in our family is 70 years old. She is a pretty, short 5'2", light-skinned woman with thinning hair. I would like for you to get to know her from a letter she wrote to our deceased mother.

Dear Mom:

As the middle girl in a family of 11 children, I felt lost when we relocated from Williston, South Carolina to Philadelphia, Pennsylvania. This transformation in itself was devastating for me since I was laughed at in school for my deep southern accent. I didn't talk much, just stayed quiet and alone. I tried hard to fit in. I even managed to have a friend or two, but I missed the South, my father, and Ezekiel; since Poppa stayed behind and Ezekiel stayed with him to help on the farm. I enjoyed singing in church and was the chief babysitter in the family for my younger siblings:

Northa (Bubbles), Hubert (Bert), Lorise and Lorine. Lorise and Lorine, my twin sisters, are extremely bad.

I am a twin to Ezekiel. Being a twin to a boy is different. We do not have to race each other. Automatically, we understand one another. The demands on girls are different from the expectations of boys. I felt mostly caught in the middle all my life. I seldom took a stand on anything.

At age 15, my older sister, Betty, ran away from home. She was my best friend and in less than two weeks at camp, she got married to the cook and left the Willis family and me far behind. After that, I had no help managing the household while you, my mother, worked doing "day work," cleaning white people's houses because, Momma, you bravely never believed in welfare or handouts.

It was hard for me because I wanted to date boys too. Now, that was impossible for me, Momma, since you didn't trust any man dating me. Momma, you became particularly hard on me. You did not want to lose me to the street gangs, marriage, or any other bad experiences. You were hurt and miserable to live with when Betty and her husband moved away to Newbury, New York.

Nonetheless, my feelings of loss were only magnified as my twin brother, Zeke, was nowhere to be found. You see, with twins, there is an unmistakable connection established before birth.

My twin brother was left behind in South Carolina. I truly needed him. I could not put my feelings into words, especially to an unaffectionate mother.

Sure, I knew you loved me, but you never kissed me or said, "I Love You." I desperately needed to hear those words. So, I rebelled against your campaign to shield me from this world. My heart was crying out for love, while America was getting more violent all the time with drugs and the civil rights movement.

You had to let me grow up, especially since I had a mind of my own. I wanted to fit in and date. Of course, I got pregnant. I had a boy child, Lawrence Anthony Willis, born on August 15, 1957. The baby's father seemed to have disappeared on me. Perhaps he was frightened of you or my six brothers. God only knows the real reason why he left me. I have another child to babysit, plus my other brothers and sisters, as well.

In those days, the church did not look favorably upon unwed mothers. I was rejected and refused membership by Thankful Baptist Church. So, I gave up my church and school, too. I became your Black sheep of the family, your example of what 'not to do.' I became defensive or abusive to the attacks from my family and society. These words burned in my very soul, each time you spoke them to me, "You ought to be ashamed of yourself. Get in there and take care of that baby. No, you can't go out. Mind your *own* baby."

I internalized everything, drowning in self-pity; numb by hurtful words and afraid to speak up and live.

In the pit of my heart, I felt frightened and alone. I still needed to hear, "I love you," spoken by someone, anyone.

I soon met another boy who, like the first one, left me with a baby. Sylvester Lee Willis was born on September 30, 1960. Determined that I would not have any more children, you marched me off to the doctor's office. Something deep inside me went cold and I never felt the same. When Zeke finally joined the family in Philadelphia, I was 18, and I felt better. But it was too late! I no longer felt a welcomed part of the Willis family. Unable to have more children – I needed a job.

I could not achieve all the success I wanted in life. One's achievements should never be measured by mistakes of the past but measured by one's character. I am a good person who made mistakes and needed to overcome adversity. I needed forgiveness. Men tricked me, society treated me with dismay, and I faced the breaking point of being humanly sane. I am truly sorry. I had enough faith to ask God for help. I made A Pact with God. "God, I need a job so I can raise my sons properly and let them grow healthy and strong. If you give me a job, I promise to make you proud of me. I'll be a strong Christian woman too, and tell others about your love for all kinds of broken folks."

God did answer my prayers, and I got a job. I worked as a maid for the Sheraton Hotel from 1960-1967. I cleaned 18 rooms and bathrooms per day, five days per week, earning $7.00 per day for a 40-hour week, or $35.00 a week. My tips were divided up between management and other housekeeping staff. Management kept valuables left in the rooms instead of returning them to me after a waiting period of 30 days. The most I got to take home was liquor. Most of the rooms I cleaned, I could not afford to rent. I did all this hard work for lousy pay. There were no paid vacations, and no time off for breaks. When employees at the Sheraton Hotel did not show up, they forced me to work at night, leaving my children alone. The whole family occasionally went to New York City by car to visit your sisters and brothers. These weekend trips were the only vacations I experienced.

Broken-hearted, riddled with guilt, depressed and surrounded by an unfriendly world, I asked God for a better job. By 1967, with God's help, I found a job making radios at Philco. They paid me $75.00 per week for 40-hours of work. I could then finally support my children. For the first time, I could also stand up to you. I contributed my share to paying the mortgage and other bills. I was still suffering because my brothers were getting married and having their children, cars, and homes, yet I struggled with raising my two children, alone, under my mother's roof in an adverse situation, as the black sheep of the family. I fought to keep my two children warm, loved and safe. Having children is like having a double-edged sword. On the one hand, you wish you never had them, but on the other hand, you love them very much. You also receive love and strength from their very existence.

In silence, my pain persisted as I saw my other siblings achieve the success of obtaining their own cars and homes. I did not. Finally, I received a helping hand from my twin Zeke; he guided me into securing my own home. No longer did I have to bear the burden of all the put-downs and negative attitudes from my family. I felt safe under my own roof.

Momma Milda and Cleveland worked at Linton's Restaurant. I remember Louis washing dishes there too. Louis always had the gift of making money. He had nice friends and side jobs, too. Louis has always been able to keep money in his pockets. There was definite upward mobility and growth happening in the Willis Family. My brothers and sisters all continued to seek higher-paying jobs.

Louis and Northa started working for Strick Trailers in Trenton, New Jersey, where they drove forklift trucks, placed lights on trailers, and worked in their paint shop. Louis was able to work from Sept 1955 - 1975, earning $9.00 per hour at 40-hours a week. Louis moved on to Progressive Lighting and made $3.50 to $13.00 per hour by 1996. John D. worked for ITT; Zeke worked for the Gas Co. as a custodian. Betty, after a failed marriage, came back home with her son, John Thomas. She finished her education and married a minister, James McLaughlin. Betty became a radio tester for Philco Computer Parts, and her son, John Thomas, worked at Philco too, before his death.

In my later years, I worked as a nurse's aide. My

baby brother, Hubert, sold newspapers as a youth and we all had to contribute to the mortgage and help buy food. Momma, you taught us the value of money. We had to save some money, be responsible, pay our bills, and straighten the cash in our wallets Cleveland, my oldest brother with the ball player dreams, pressed flyers, worked at Linton's as a dishwasher and then worked at the Electric Company. Cleveland later became a City Councilman. All this progress came to us because the Willis family moved to Philadelphia to improve their situations for the better.

Although I might have been the black sheep of the family, today I am a happy grandmother. I live near my sons, who are hard-working individuals. Mother, I did not do so badly. Sorry if we did not always get along, but I understand that the journey from slavery to becoming a whole person was not an easy one.

Love, Zenobia

P.S.: Bubbles became a drug counselor. We have college graduates in our family now. Bubbles, Lorine, and Lorise all have graduate degrees, too. All from a woman who had a sixth-grade education and raised 11 children, all by herself.

Almost all my brothers and sisters are retired now after years of hard work and raising wonderful children. They all prospered in a system where Black people were often the first fired and the last hired, where prejudice and discrimination were the norms.

Zenobia's story is vital to the endurance of mankind, as it shows that even the weakest of humans can become the strongest if they have a desire to succeed. My brother, Louis' story, brings reality to the character of the men in the Willis family.

CHAPTER 10
Louis' story

One's faith in God is always rewarded.

When doing research, you can often expect the unexpected. That's what happened when I interviewed Louis, my 78-year-old brother.

"Tell me a story about our Father. I really don't remember him since he died when I was four," I asked him.

Louis' coarse voice slowly started.

"Leaving from South Carolina to Pennsylvania was no easy thing to do." He paused much longer than I expected. His strong, handsome face made a striking silhouette in the soft evening dusk. He seemed to be thinking.

"Well, I remember we had to kill three to four hogs every year to survive from July to next August. Then we took the meat and let it cure for six to eight weeks in a smoke-house – that process gave us three to four boxes of pork. That meat became sausage, country bacon, and cured hams. This would last 'til Easter. We put the meat we took from the smoke-house into the icebox. This process became such a pleasure for me. Eating meat daily was a luxury that we didn't have. This was our opportunity to have our own variety of meat, albeit pork, for any sustained period

John D. and I milked the cows every morning at first light and that even added milk to our meals. We knew how to put the milk in the icebox and pack it with ice. Cream would always rise to the top of the milk.

"Momma would skim the cream off the top and churn three pounds of butter every day. We sold butter to the neighbors for $.10 or $.15 a pound and ate it on tender corn-bread, finger-licking flapjacks, buttermilk biscuits, and sweet bread that Momma made. The rest of the dough used to make sweet bread, was left to swell into fluffy rolls overnight. Thirteen pieces of bacon came from a slab of the pork. Nothing was better than bacon or sausages and eggs with grits.

"On Sundays, we killed two chickens for dinner. We tried hard to make our food stretch until August, so, sometimes we hunted for rabbits because squirrels were too quick for us to catch. Possums were good to eat, but raccoon (when the law allowed us to kill them), was my favorite meat. It was brown and lean and tasty. When we used our hunting catch of the day, only one chicken would be killed that Sunday. We even had a fish pond. We trapped three to five of the fish to cook almost every day. When hunting failed, and the crops and vegetables died out from the drought, we fished for white perch, sea trout, and catfish. Momma used turtles to make turtle soup. Our fried catfish just melted in my mouth and there were big pieces, too. We ate rice every day. As a part of our history, persons who were descendants of Africans who were enslaved on the rice plantations were called Geechees. Many of these descendants came from the rice-growing region of West Africa. Because rice was a staple part of our daily diet, in South Carolina, we are known as *Geechees*. Momma was a great cook and stretched our food to make it last. The way she fried chicken made it crispy, and it tasted sweet."

"After a long day's work, working from sun up to sun down on our rented 80 acres of land, Poppa insisted that all 13 family members eat at the same table at the same time. We always had to hold hands and bless the food and nothing was allowed to be left on our plates."

"Sometimes, Daddy farmed out John D. and me (I mean sub-contracted us to work for others), because we could not pay our bills when we finished our crops. We worked for Ed Christ, who paid me $1.50 per day, and I worked 5 1/2 days per week. I picked cotton like a machine, walking on my knees and pulling a heavy sack full of cotton behind me. My hands soon became coarse from being pricked by hard, pointy cotton stems and the sun would beat down on my poor, weak body. But, I kept plodding along without anger while planting string beans, sweet potatoes, and watermelons, knowing I was helping my family out. I had to give Momma the money, and she would give me back $1.50. In those days, a movie cost five cents, popcorn cost a nickel a box and I got a nickel to give to the church. Sometimes when I gave Poppa the money I made –he'd give me a whole dollar from the ten dollars I would give him. Still, I liked to give my earnings to Momma."

"Once a week, we would heat the water on the stove to fill a number three tub (the larger tub) to take our baths. Two kids took baths together while we played and laughed and were rushed to get out so the others could take their baths. After we got dressed, we attended St. Peter's Church about one mile from home. Our real church was Ebenezer Baptist Church, about twenty miles away in Aiken, South Carolina. Back then, every child under 12 years old would stay home and care for the farm. The only reason I couldn't go to church was that I didn't have a suit. First, the hand- me-downs went from Poppa to Glover Cleveland, Jr., my oldest brother, to John D., then to me. In a few years, my growth caught up with John D., and we finally had to wear the same suit. I wore John D.'s suit when John D. didn't need it. I used it when I saw my girlfriend and when I went to church."

"Momma wanted out of that bad situation that kept us defeated – especially when we all went to bed hungry, no matter how hard we worked every day. We never seemed to be happy and relaxed. During that time, nine-month-old John Thomas died of malnutrition. Then, my oldest sister, Mildred, got married because the family couldn't feed her. Then the baby of the family, you Lorine, almost died from Rickets. It was some kind of vitamin D deficiency from mal-nutrition, so the doctors said."

"About that time, Mildred promised us a better life and that was about when Momma needed her dreams to come true. Her sisters had migrated to New York City and some of Poppa's family had moved from South Carolina to Chester, Pennsylvania. A neighbor, Deacon Paul, took us to the train station and Momma prayed;

"Lord, we have to step out on faith." Momma knew God personally. She kept on praying, "GOD! You know the Pact I have with You. . . I'll give you all my children and praise your name if you keep them safe and well-fed. So, I'm calling on You now to honor our Pact. God, I need a change. I'm tired of trying to feed my children, tired of all the hard work," she said as tears were rolling down her full cheeks."

"Momma was at the end of her rope, I mean, she was tired of begging and scraping to just survive in South Carolina. She didn't have money to pay for Hubert, you, your twin, Lorise; Zenobia, Betty, John, me and herself to pay for the train ride to meet Mildred and Grover Cleveland, Jr. in Philadelphia."

"Momma cried out to God, "God, I need you now!"

Louis looked at me as if he were a cat swallowing the canary. He swallowed hard, then continued to tell history. "The fare was twenty dollars and Momma had only $11.00. Anyone having gold coins was supposed to turn them in. Poppa had planned to give each child one gold piece and a milking cow on his or her wedding day. Momma's heart became so heavy and her hands was so hot because she was cashing in our inheritance. She slowly and carefully handed the banker one silver dollar. He gave her back five dollars in change. The gold piece had brought her six dollars. That was $11.00 for the gold and silver coins. Those 1836 silver and gold dollar pieces were worth double what she got for them. They were worth five thousand dollars. I yanked at her coat sleeve."

"I am sorry I didn't turn them in sooner," Momma said, looking like she was afraid of being arrested.

The banker yelled at her, "Just get out of here!" He smiled after placing his newly found wealth in his pockets. I pulled at her coat sleeve again."

"Momma, I hid my money under the mattress and saved up thirty-six dollars from the dollar-fifty a week you gave me back from my work in the fields."

'Momma bent down and looked me straight in my eyes, holding me, "Boy, don't you play with me or I'll slap you blind.'

"My shoulders trembled between her hands; "No, Momma, I got thirty-six dollars, and you can have it. I spent only the fifty-cents every week. I saved the rest."

"Momma tightened her grip on me, crying aloud until I thought I would break. But I saw joyful tears rolling from both eyes down a tired face. I had saved the day. Thank God!"

"When we reached Philadelphia, Aunt Ceolda (Momma's baby sister); and my father's brother; that lived in from Chester, PA, made sure that I got my *own* suit, shoes, and other clothes. We all went about adjusting to life in the city."

"Poppa came for Christmas and we all enjoyed every minute of him being with us. He wore his one-piece long johns, and we laughed that he was only comfortable in the upstairs bathroom where it was cooler. In three months, he told us the land needed his attention. So, he returned to South Carolina to plant the crops. A month later, we got word that he had sunstroke and died. Poppa's plans to give us one milk cow and a gold piece each when we got married went wrong– our legacy was gone forever, along with his dreams for his family. Momma was more determined than ever that the family would not die along with our Poppa."

Instead of a story, Louis gave me wisdom, the proud plan our father had for us. All my life, I had believed that Poppa didn't want his family living in Philadelphia. That he abandoned us, but that wasn't true. It was just the shape of Black people's lives following three generations after slavery. Laws and votes never ceased to make a hard life easier. I really thanked Louis for giving me that piece of the puzzle. Louis' story will be in my heart forever. My praying mother was at a crossroads in her life. Looking back, she faced poverty and destruction, but looking forward was the "Promised Land," hope and opportunity.

With luggage tied with strings and the best of her fried chicken, she ventured forth toward our new life. From that day on, when I would have fear in my heart, I'd stand tall on faith as my Momma had done over and over again. We all have crossroads in our lives, but believing in God can create peace and understanding. The entire Willis family had to learn to navigate through this new "Promised Land."

CHAPTER 11

Education

The challenge is not obtaining an education, but educating oneself by living honorably.

Lorise and I learned to memorize books as small kids. We could recite poetry and parts of *The Bible*. We often challenged each other to learn school work and competed to get the best grades. Although we attended an integrated elementary school; but junior high school and high school were totally segregated. The education they provided was below par. I often heard that teachers were instructed not to teach the required state curriculum. They paid Black teachers to share only one half of the curriculum. All books and facilities were hand-me-downs from white schools. We still had to work hard to learn from what had been given to us. In most of the Black schools, it was dangerous to use the bathrooms because of possibly catching bacteria from old urine or faeces, or being attacked by some bully who had it "in" for you. Students locally couldn't even use school restrooms in some Black schools.

My twin and I were allowed the luxury of not working while attending school. Although we didn't get the best grades, we were good students with perfect attendance records. We enjoyed school and loved to compete while studying. We even competed with our weight and height.

As a part of our subjects, Lorise and I also did some typing because we knew it was necessary if we were to work in any type of office. As a matter of fact, having typing without some of the other subjects wouldn't be a bad idea since you could still get an office job. Our older sisters, Betty and Zenobia, didn't do as well, as they never learned to type.

It was a constant thing for Lorise and me to compete for everything, even dates. Once when we were seventeen, they had a party in the school gym and I had to change my clothes right there in the gym.

"Look at her changing," laughed a girl near the door. "She always changes," another voice said.

Lorise and I moved on and scanned the room, searching for potential dates. The first person each of us talked to was off-limits for the other twin. We only broke that rule on a few occasions. One of those occasions was when I felt alone and abandoned. I was a normal teenager who was uncomfortable with my identity, thinking my twin sister was prettier than me. But I saw cute Buddy Smith at the same second as Lorise.

"He's mine," Lorise and I said at the same time. We had a fight about it, but after the party, neither of us mentioned him again, neither did we see him again after summer school.

We also became Queens of our junior high school, and we twisted around the school like Chubby Checker. But in the real world, Lorise and I were separated and didn't have even one class together. We couldn't wait to get home to compare notes.

People we didn't even know accused us of being stuck-up. You see, they would speak first and then we would speak in return. Lorise knew half the school and I knew the other half. We would often need to inform the person addressing us that they had mixed up one of us for the other twin sister, but they wouldn't believe us. We gained popularity in the wrong way.

As our school life progressed; it became real to us that one half of the world had great hearts and the other half either didn't know or learn what the real world was about. What it really was about was Lorise and me not realizing that we didn't have a good education.

While at school, we all lived in fear of war – the air raid drills, the fire drills and talks of communism and a Cuban bomb.

Then, suddenly, all our leaders were being assassinated. JFK DIES. — I sat frozen at my desk. Then the loudspeaker called us all into the gym and announced that John F. Kennedy had been shot and killed. Young ladies and men were not prepared for that much sadness, fear and loss. He was the first President young enough to engage our imagination with a sense of approachability. No, that couldn't be true. John F. "Jack" Kennedy, born May 29, 1917, died November 22, 1963, was the 35th President of the United States. JFK will always be "ingrained" into my brain.

I covered myself in a vast blanket of sadness. Some students cried; some could not. I was one who could not cry or even speak. The country lost its innocence. A roll of murderous terror seemed to permanently attach itself to our nation.

Robert F. "Bobby" Kennedy, the younger brother of the late President John F. Kennedy, was born November 20, 1925; and was shot and killed on June 6, 1968. RFK served as the U.S. Attorney General, 1961 to 1964.

Those Kennedy brothers touched the consciousness of the people to consider the Civil Rights Law of 1964, and I will always feel the power of that movement. The Bill had been introduced to America in John F. Kennedy's speech on June 11, 1963. We learned that John and Robert Kennedy's ideals of Civil Rights Law were going to be carried forward by JFK's successor, Lyndon B. Johnson. JFK and RFK contributed significantly to my understanding and consciousness of the Civil Rights Movement. Those two were and would continue to be a tremendous part of my history and my future.

CHAPTER 12
High School Days

Three kinds of trust; Trust in God, Trust in Man and Trust in a Loved one.

Simon Gratz High School was a large, red-brick building that covered the entire block, along with Gillespie Jr. High School. The school had every club activity a student could ask for, and they were on our schedule. Now that Lorise was in my classes and the reputation spread about our six brothers, nobody bothered us because our watchdogs were always around. The Willis boys seemed to be everywhere at all times. Turn a corner and there was a brother. Close a locker, another brother popped up. It was like magic. My brothers were using their ESP to keep tabs on us.

At times that protection was rough. Our brothers teased us about having pencils in our shoes instead of legs as our legs were so thin. Besides what was taking place in history, high school was a relatively happy time, except that I learned the school district gave our mother the task of teaching us when she only had a sixth-grade education. Making the best out of a bad situation, my mother encouraged us to join every extra-

Lorine W. Calhoun

curricular activity offered at Simon Gratz High School:
Student Association Representatives, Better Speech Club, 12B
Club, Officers' Club, V.P., Monitors, Year book, Spotlight
School Newspapers (co-editors), The World Affairs Club, Red
Cross Club, Five Foot-Femmes, The Chess Club, Library
Aides, Cabinet Representatives, Lunch-room Aides,
Counselor's Aides, Commerce Club, Prom Committee, Roster
Officer Aides, Pin Committee, and finally the Banquet
Committee.

My twin sister and I always found ourselves as President
and Co-president in one or more of those organizations. We
both participated in the high school musical, *Hello Dolly.*
We both loved it. We giggled every day after rehearsals. The
prediction was that Lorise and Lorine Willis would be in
Hollywood doing the *Double Mint* commercial. We were
voted "Most Popular" and won "Golden Pens" at graduation.
It was a good thing we had been forced to take speech classes
to correct our deep southern accents. It certainly helped with
the acting and the writing, after all. Although there might have
been drugs and gangs on campus, I didn't see any. Yes, life
was excellent. At home was another story.

After Zenobia's pregnancy at 16, Momma provided more
structure for Lorise and I. She didn't want the same thing to
happen to us that happened to Zenobia. After school, church
became our second home. We'd march down there three times
a week at 8:00 a.m., -Sunday School; and at 11:00 a.m.-
services. We were ushers, made announcements and recited
the welcome address in unison. On Wednesday nights, we
practiced Twin Modeling Classes. Saturdays brought
Missionary Club and Jr. Progressive Club, where we supplied

65

flowers for the church. Momma was in the Adult Progressive Club that met on Sundays after service. This meant we couldn't leave until all her meetings were over and we'd be in church until 2:00 p.m., then came afternoon and night services. Sunday was God's Day at church all day long. I even got married in a Tom Thumb Wedding.

I also participated in plays with my mother every year for Mother's Day and Thanksgiving. We did a Convention too. Momma loved the applause. Our religion didn't allow dancing much like the movie *Footloose,* but plays were just fine. I wondered about that for the longest time. Having fun one way was the same as having fun another way. Oh, well...

One day, out of the blue, Lorise whispered to me, "You're always forcing me to wear sexy clothes and I don't like it."

"You crazy. Momma lets both of us choose. You never say anything when she asks you. You can say something." I said.

She tossed her head and switched off. What did it matter anyhow? Dating would be out of the picture until we got to be 17. So, in the meantime, we just decided to occupy our time by tricking people who came to the house. We'd trick them with our names, making them guess who was who, then laughed at their mistakes.

At school, we were also schemers. Teachers usually put one of us at the back of the classroom and one at the front. Then they would announce, "One twin deserves a 'B' and the other a 'C' but I am giving them both B's because their names are so similar and I can't tell them apart." We just smiled.

During those years, of both our junior high and high school, and although we knew how we felt, the Civil Rights

Lorine W. Calhoun

Movement was too adult for us to discuss until we graduated from high school. We however felt a bit afraid of what was happening in the South, especially at the Walgreens (where coloreds could not be served at the lunch counter) just a mile away. I was looking forward to my personal life growing as a teen; and I had no idea what that looked like. When doubt came, I always had to face my pact with God. Somehow, I knew it would turn out alright.

CHAPTER 13
Higher Education

Higher Education is not for cowards, especially in Philadelphia.

My brothers and sisters all had to get jobs before they finished high school instead of preparing for college or going into sports or some money-making vocation. It started in slavery and had inched its way into my life, three generations later. Just because white plantation owners disallowed my ancestors to read, write and learn numbers, was no reason for me to sit there and accept it so many years later. I would break that curse! The more I heard about the Movement, the more I wanted to break out of ignorance and poverty.

During that sweltering summer after high school, we looked for jobs in the mornings and sat around talking about discrimination in the afternoons. We grumbled about the twisted views that employers had about Black people; views that held us back as a race. When the burden of all that talk got to be too much for us, we'd find one of our teachers and talk to them because we figured that none of our thoughts or questions would be answered in a history book.

After one of my job-hunting Wednesday mornings, I ran into one of my teachers who took me to lunch and brought up the subject of Mr. Scokley. He turned out to be a man who wanted to attend the University of Chicago Medical School to become a medical doctor in 1939. But, when the Black man appeared at the registration office in person for his interview, the Board of Trustees turned him down. He fought back and ultimately entered and graduated. That school never recognized him as a doctor. Years later, he died selling hair products in Philadelphia. I decided right then that the same predicament wasn't going to happen to me. Some Blacks only sat back and watched the news and waited for things to change on their own. Whites said we were moving too fast. Then came, the Black Power Movement.

We all had opinions and spewed them out, coming and going. Advocates of Black Power argued that integration robs African Americans of their common heritage, dignity and economy. Even the term "Black Power" seemed to scare both white and Black people alike. It meant standing up and becoming owners of businesses, taking charge of seeing that their children got an equitable education and being aware of law and order. Opinions about racism reached worldwide. One popular opinion was that Blacks in the United States did not assimilate well into the "mainstream" culture. I wasn't sure, but it wasn't my desire – yet I didn't want to be relegated to poverty and ignorance either.

One of the most public symbols of the Black Power Movement was born at the 1968 Olympics when two African-Americans stood together in a defiant position on the podium and raised their fists, Tommie Smith and John Carlos. That one act resonated around the world. It was a moment in history. The Black Power Salute was duplicated by Black teenagers, men and women and even foreign Blacks all over the world. It was a powerful time of solidarity for African Americans, a unifying song being sung in concert. The country was filled with the heat of unified fervor.

I had just finished high school with students who were moving toward making a name for themselves: Patty La-Belle, the actress and singer; winner of Grammy Awards, the NAACP Image Award, American Music Awards and The Soul Train Award. Tammy Terrell or Tammy Montgomery, who sang with Marvin Gaye, had been in my music class. William Gray, another classmate, who had headed the United Negro College Fund became a minister, a U.S. Congressman in 1978, and Majority Whip in 1989. I graduated with Tyrone Beverly, brother of Frankie Beverly of the famous Frankie Beverly and Maze. The Delfonics Doo Wop group, sang at my high school, their popular song 'La La Means I Love You.' Their 'Didn't I Blow Your Mind This Time,' was used on the soundtrack of Quentin Tarantino's film, *Jackie Brown*.

At graduation, I had a feeling of grandeur, a euphoric feeling. Do you remember high school when you graduated and thought you could conquer the world, or at least change the world? Well, I had a stark awakening only weeks later, when I started looking for a job. It was then I realized that the magic dust of graduation had worn off, and the blinders were removed from my eyes. I saw the reality of how far I had been setback. But I was not prepared to let that stop me. My grammar was poor and my math aptitude was below average.

Immediately I enrolled in the neighborhood tutoring program and night school. In three months, I increased my shorthand speed and did everything I could to become "job-ready." I was determined! There was a thirst in my heart and an intentionality in my mind!

Life, as I saw it, was messed up with the Vietnam War, the Civil Rights Movement, drugs and gangs. We must have sung too many victory songs and they all settled in our heads and not our hearts. I could be successful because I had a Pact with God and He wouldn't allow anything to stop me. I was going to make something out of my life – no bad background, poor education, or low self-esteem could stop me. I believed in Langston Hughes' (poet, novelist, playwright, activist) piece of work called A Dream Deferred:

A Dream Deferred

When a dream is deferred, God cries a tear. First, He sees what you can accomplish. Second, He sees you can fail. But in the middle of His teardrop, we see His love. We all had dreams after high school. Our parents had a good dream for us too, no matter how they showed it. Everyone has a story that we can learn from. All those deferred dreams, yet life can still be wonderful.

CHAPTER 14
First Jobs

Sometimes things are too good to be true. Choose to ride waves of positivity forever.

In 1965, my twin sister Lorise and I were standing on the main street in downtown Philadelphia, laughing and talking. Suddenly, I noticed the tall buildings that seemed to swell with the possibility of work. Soon we found ourselves in front of Reliance Insurance Company looking up at its 22 floors. A tall, good-looking Black man in a chauffeur's uniform beckoned to us. Then he pointed to the building.

"Go in there and tell them you're Sydney Williams' cousin." We looked at him with a confused look on our faces.

"They turned down a hundred and one girls for those few jobs today. Go on in there now."

"Thank you, Sir," we sang, and took off toward the elevator. Inside the interviewing office, we announced our cousin, the chauffeur; and of course, we got the jobs. Even we were surprised that Sydney Williams was telling the truth. But we found out that he was chauffeur to Mr. Robert Gill,

President of Reliance Insurance Company. But the awesome part of the story didn't end there. The manager wasted no time putting us to work. Lorise was sent to the next floor to work, and I was taken to the cubby hole in the corner and taught to file by numbers. The inside two numbers, then the outside two and lastly the last two digits. This Reliance Insurance Company job was modern-day slavery. A performance expert had just installed a new filing system and each file clerk had to file folders by the clock.

In the next three days, I contracted the flu and was too sick to work. In the time that I was gone, they transferred me to a different department to save my job. After three days in my new department, I was given a birthday party and I cried like a newborn baby. I never had a cake of my very own without my twin sister's name on it, too. But my happiness was short-lived. For lunch, I was given green split pea soup to get rid of my cold. That soup came right back up and I was out like a light terminated. I didn't last two weeks on that job. I still will not eat green split pea soup, even today.

I was determined that life wouldn't stop me. On my next job, I had to type hundreds of March of Dimes and other companies' cards every day. I didn't last two weeks, typing by the clock. My self-esteem was in the tank. I felt low and inadequate. I couldn't type or file, and certainly not both of them. So, I decided to volunteer. No one could be fired from volunteering. But, to make matters worse, Lorise kept her job at Reliance Insurance Company. I resented her for keeping that job. She was able to work under the pressure of doing three people's work to hold on to that $50.00 a week job. She held her head up high.

Lorine W. Calhoun

At the Opportunities Industrialization Center (OIC), the local minister, Reverend Leon H. Sullivan, turned grant money into a center to train people for jobs. I marched right down there and volunteered for two months. Then I learned that instead of hiring four volunteers, they had hired eight part-time people. Well, I got mad and wanted to quit.

I told management, "I want a job and I need a job. I deserve to be full time. I am younger and faster than the other workers."

There, I was able to practice my typing and filing skills. I advanced so fast that I was a volunteer for the least amount of time ever in OIC history. Reverend Leon H. Sullivan's book, '*Build, Brother, Build,*' even included my picture. Furthermore, I was making more money than my sister Lorise. Lorise, of course, got jealous. She applied for a job where I worked and got hired in the International Office. I worked at the local OIC Feeder Program, On-the-Job-Training and the Adult Armchair Education Program for six years. Lorise worked at International for ten years. She made more money than I did, again! But the lesson here is that I kept seeking a job until I found a job that lasted. With that blessing, my confidence returned and lodged in my heart.

Lorise and I were 19-years-old and had made it past the 17-year-old pregnancy curse. Momma was always checking underwear for monthly menstrual periods, waiting up all night for curfew and making sure church attendance was excellent. She watched our every move and ran off every boyfriend who looked like he might become a serious love interest.

The dating game was hard. We didn't get to keep boyfriends and we were sexually inactive. We were sheltered by six brothers and one worried mother who made sure boys didn't get too close.

While girlfriends envied and admired us, they really didn't know the truth about our dating lives; boyfriends were few – the few we had needed to get along with our six brothers and our mother as well. Still, I was searching for happiness when I didn't know what it was; I was seeking it in a world that was not always happy. I listened when my Momma would say, "If you make rash decisions based on hot temptation, you'll pay the price." I wondered what the heck she was talking about. Little did I know I'd soon find out.

CHAPTER 15
The Wedding

With no manual on love, humans make mistakes and carry heavy regrets.

An OIC office Christmas party was thickly laid out with balloons, food, and egg-nog that smelled rich like vanilla. The laughter melted into "My Girl" by the Temptations when Lorise and I walked in. The strapping, nice-looking young man was coming straight toward me, wearing a tiny smile on his lips. I quickly decided he wasn't my type–tall, dark, and handsome was my ratio. But, by the time we were face-to-face, he was in a full smile. His eyes were soft and easy and he had a comforting voice.

"Hi," he said. "Hello," I answered.

"You're downright pretty," he said. "I don't mean no disrespect…"

Strolling toward the punch bowl, we exchanged living locations and job history. He cocked his head and took my hand.

"Give me your phone number. I want to talk to you some more."

"What's your name," I asked.

"Peter Calhoun," he said, releasing my hand. The name "Calhoun" had me laughing. The only Calhoun I knew was Lawyer Calhoun on the Amos and Andy Show – a Black sitcom on television. I didn't particularly like that name, but I gave him my phone number, and a shiver came over me.

Over the next few days, Peter Calhoun called me every day and we talked for hours. He read me poetry and imitated Calhoun on the TV Show. I began to wait for his calls.

Have you ever seen someone possessed? Well, that's what I saw when I introduced my mother to Peter Calhoun. For the first time in my life, I saw my mother, Ruth, in a different light. She did a war dance, pointed her fingers in Pete's face, jumped up and down and shouted, "That is the one, that is the o-n -e!"

Momma had lost her mind. Well, after that, I composed myself, scratched my head and wondered what alien had taken over my mother's body and mind. I wondered how long it would be before she started acting her normal self again. Right then, she started up again.

"The Lord says, *this man* is gonna be in our lives for years to come!"

War dance or not, Mr. Peter Calhoun started "being" in our lives more and more. He had two sisters, Mae and Mattie. His mother, Evelyn, seemed nice, but Peter's father, Peter Calhoun, Sr., drank too much.

I noticed that Momma didn't mind him picking me up. Pete picked me up in his 1965, jet blue convertible Corvair. When we were a safe distance from the house, he'd take a drink from a flask in his pocket. It couldn't be too bad since my mother's boyfriend, Stoney, a preacher, drank too.

Pete and I went everywhere together. That five-foot, nine-inch, poetry reading Romeo, had an intellectual side to him, too. He was about to graduate, in Accounting, from La-Salle College. He was looking better all the time. He was an athlete while attending Simon Gratz High School, the same school my older sisters and brother had attended. With those romantic rides in his car with the top down and poetry and small gifts, I got hooked on Peter Calhoun, Jr.

My sister, Betty, said she was concerned as Pete had been her classmate, which meant he was nine-years-older than me.

"I like him a lot," I said, brushing her off. I finally had someone to love me. Even my mother and brothers couldn't frighten him off from dating me like they did my other boyfriends. By that time, Momma decided I was not her favorite twin.

"So be it," I said to myself. Now when Lorise and I were near each other, she would yell without me even touching her. Momma would jump on Lorise's side and yell at me. I was rebelling and wanted out of being a twin. All the bragging, showing off pictures, discussions of who was the favorite were over for me. I was tired of it and besides, I had Peter Calhoun.

Once I dated a tall, handsome guy who lived near my home. We went for a ride to Cape May, New Jersey, then turned around and drove back home. We got home really late, about 2:00 o'clock in the morning with only a smack on the lips when we parted. Well, the family decided he was mentally ill and I was never to see Barry Thomas again. How could a big brother to needy kids and who owned his own car be mentally ill? He didn't seem mentally ill to me. Well, after that innocent night, I was forced to go to the doctor for an exam.

A gynecologist examination to a virgin is scary and painful as I had to spread my body on a cold table, take off all my clothes and cover myself with only a thin white sheet. The silver stirrups felt cold against my bare feet. Then, something that felt like a cold iron pushed inside my body. I screamed while my mother looked on. What the hell was the doctor doing?

"She's alright. No signs of sex," the doctor said.

My mother smiled triumphantly. How could I stop an overbearing mother? I had begun to plot in my mind just how to do that. After attending about 100 weddings of friends and family members, I stood in line to catch a bouquet. It was Gwen and Joe Stout's wedding where I reached up and knocked down the bride to catch the bouquet. That meant good luck and I would be sure to become the next girl to marry. Well, at least Lorise was dating her high school sweetheart, who took her to the prom, so how could I be the next one to get married?

David, on the other hand, gave me a birthday party at his apartment for Lorise and me. My mother took one look at this dark, handsome musician who played the bass fiddle and said, "You been married before, haven't you?"

David dropped his head and answered, "Yes."

"Get out and don't come back!" Momma yelled. That took care of David forever. But as for me, that scene would replay in my mind forever; as I remembered my mother's actions every time I introduced her to a new love interest.

Although I didn't see marriage in the picture for me at all, I needed a bad boy to stand up to my mother and my six brothers. So, Mr. Peter Calhoun would have to do. He was on Navy disability retirement of 50%. This situation was due for a re-evaluation in five years. Pete was retired for an oversized heart, a nervous condition and arthritis of the ankles. He seemed to come from a decent family. His retirement from the Navy meant security for me as we would never have to pay medical bills. Also, being able to travel almost anywhere in the world on military standby was another plus.

Pete received a small pension and lastly, because of the GI Bill, he could continue getting a higher education. One day in my mother's kitchen, I was washing dishes and Peter was drying them. Suddenly, he dropped to one knee and looked up at me and said, "Will you marry me?"

Without much thought, I said, "Yes." I was in love, in a dream world and a dreamland since I didn't really know what love meant. Pete had two sisters and a mother that loved the ground he walked on; and now I was watching and taking on their emotions. I loved Peter too.

Friends and church members did not believe I was breaking up "the twin thing." What will your sister do without you? That was a silly question. I was only getting married, not dying.

In the month that followed, I picked out a 3/4 karat diamond ring with a cathedral setting of white gold. Now, the next big issue faced me – sex. I was embarrassed that I had to ask the people at work about making love. It was so confusing to me. In the movie theater, I peeked and the different positions confused me, too. Oh, I worked at the Registration Department of OIC and asked for advice from a 35-year-old who never married. She was a single mother. They all laughed and said, "Give him some sex because you are already engaged!"

So, taking their advice, we had our first love encounter at his efficiency apartment. The quiet privacy didn't make things any better for me. I felt nervous and remembered that doctor's exam my mother forced on me. It hurt when he entered my body. My first experience having sex was no longer a mystery and definitely not enjoyable. I felt that it would get better with practice, with more time together. No one in the family said anything about our late nights together, or tried breaking us up. Only, stories started about Pete not being stable. There were rumors of him needing medicine. These rumors were coming to a happy woman. They were not acceptable because I had fallen in love.

Then, two weeks before the wedding, the invitations were mailed out and all the preparations were ready. Peter Calhoun took my sisters Zenobia, Lorise, and me on a drunken car ride, weaving in and out the streets of Philadelphia. Zenobia was trembling when she whispered, "What are you going to do?"

"Nothing," I said.

Lorise shook her head, "No. You have to do something."

I paid no attention to this sign of disaster. Instead, I chose a dining room, living room and bedroom set, and placed it all on layaway. I negotiated the price down to their bare minimum and scheduled payments. Peter purchased a triplex on Penn Street, three doors down from Pete's efficiency apartment. I chose the girls that grew up with me to be my six bridesmaids and Pete's sister, Mattie, as the Matron of Honor. I wanted a pastel wedding. Each girl had her own color and her own gown. Since they were paying for them, I didn't care what they looked like. I hated the empire dresses the girls chose, but the bridesmaids loved them. I only tried on two wedding gowns. The second one was the most beautiful gown I had ever seen. The long white dress had lace and pearls, with an Aline fitted skirt, lacy sleeves, and a long train. The headdress was rich in lace and pearls with a beautiful net veil hanging to the waist.

It was five months after meeting Mr. Peter Calhoun, Jr., on Saturday, September 16, 1967, at 1:00 p.m. on my wedding day. it rained; I mean, it poured that morning. I received several calls regarding the rain which I could do nothing about. I politely told the callers that it had to be some type of weather, didn't it? Well, the weather cleared up in time for the wedding and I was still in dreamland. My mother came to the dressing room and looked me in the eyes. "If you are getting married to spite me, please don't do it."

I looked straight in her eyes and said simply, "No, Momma, I love him."

The men all wore black tuxedos with striped ties and cummerbunds. Thankful that the Baptist Church, in which I grew up had long white bows at the pews and a white sheeted-carpet spread out on which the bride would walk down the aisle. My six bridesmaids, six groomsmen, Lorise, my maid of honor, and Mattie, my matron of honor, were all excited for us. My favorite Uncle W. "Bill" Willis, my father's brother, gave me away. It was very special to him since he had never been married. The only hitch was that the groomsmen and my husband all smelled like a liquor distillery from partying. It was a bad omen.

We all danced in the rented hall and the groom provided all the liquor while my family and friends provided all the food. Ella, the wedding planner, had the hall decorated with a beautiful long wedding table and a section for the family. Momma put together the best wedding Thankful Baptist Church had ever seen. Five hundred people attended, in spite of the downpour that morning. After the reception, I changed into my custom white silk suit and Peter escorted me to our 1965 blue Corvair car. We drove toward Chicago, Illinois, for our four-day honeymoon. I couldn't have been happier. Stars were in the daylight, in my hair, and on my face. My heart pumped with sheer joy.

I was annoyed, though, that below the surface of my loving heart, I felt a warning, a sadness, a deep-down loneliness. That had to be nothing but the leftovers from years of living with my controlling mother. I smiled and kissed Peter Calhoun on the neck.

"What's that one for?" "Just because I love you." He smiled and kept driving.

CHAPTER 16

The Honeymoon

Happiness is a colorful, rare treasure.

Once we reached the hotel we went out to explore the surroundings. We took pictures in front of the lakes and fountains. We took hundreds of photos and loved looking good. We got dressed for dinner and people asked if we were movie stars. We sure felt like stars. My man, my husband, could walk on water.

I stretched out the honeymoon with a one-month anniversary and a two-month anniversary also. Anyone coming to the house should have called first as they always caught us in bed. We were truly in love. We barely attended functions as we were in love and never arrived on time, anyway.

Now that the reality of life bullied its way back into our daily lives, the hint of regret rose in my chest again. It was just a touch of loneliness. Then, one day, I found that Pete had taken $6,000 that I had saved from working at OIC and paid it down on a triplex where we could rent out the second and third floors. It didn't seem to bother him that I was upset. He moved ahead and applied for a small business loan to start his own business. Then he graduated from LaSalle College and received a degree in Business Administration.

No one told us that we needed to support ourselves in order to live. I was green about finances. Peter handled the taxes, bills and insurance policies also. He knew at all times how much money was in my wallet. Pete taught me how to cook, too. Now, the sadness rose full-fledged in my chest.

I vividly remembered when Betty had warned me that I was marrying someone she went to school with.

"Pete is mean-spirited," she said. "Two mean people will not make it," my sister Mildred said. "Taking your money will never be enough.

Sure enough, Peter started acting jealous. We were invited to a special pre-engagement party. It was a beautiful party with a lot of Nat King Cole crooning. While Peter was talking with some friend, a buddy of mine took my hand and we began to dance. I was happy that Peter took this opportunity to speak and show that he was the smartest person in the room. Others gathered around them and joined in. He looked so animated while being important.

When one guy shouted him down with a few added facts concerning the history of the Black Panther Movement, he jerked away from the group and headed straight towards me. He yanked my hands off my buddy's shoulder and dragged me out the door behind him. I never got to thank the host for the invitation. I guess I was too scared and embarrassed to do that anyhow. He begged his way back into my arms, and I felt close to him again. Yet I realized that he was nine years older than me since his acting up was now becoming a problem. I started noticing that if he couldn't be the center of attention, he would suddenly leave in a disappointed fashion, especially if someone said something more intelligent than him.

Life rolled forward and we fell back into our daily, loving routine. When Pete opened his own Public Accounting Office, a three-story building on 22nd Street in North Philadelphia, I worked at OIC to pay the rent. I was determined to become somebody. I was destined to beat the left-overs of slavery. We had a grand opening and our tenant, an exterminator, took the credit for owning the building. You know life is strange and people don't mind taking credit for your achievements or pushing you out of the way to build their self-esteem.

I had to co-sign for everything since I was the only one with a job. I signed for a 1969 Ford RT car and small business loans and insurance policies. Now, if you think I did not love my husband, you are crazy. He was my first sexual partner and I was in a perfect marriage. It had to be perfect. I remember when Momma said God sent him. Did she hear God, right? Maybe. Maybe not. I only knew that I was beginning to feel sick whenever he was near me. I sometimes chastised myself for marrying him. My mother gave us food and his mother gave him money. Life is about choices, and we may regret the choices we make all our natural lives. After all of my careful choices, under my mother's watchful eyes, it seemed that my genetics, my background and the country life had readily joined forces. Then, these all resonated in my world to support what I hoped would be the perfect marriage.

CHAPTER 17

Till Death Do Us Part

Two people in love can conquer the world if they are united as one.

The wonderful honeymoon in Chicago on September 23, 1967, had long since faded and I wondered what the hell I did by marrying Pete Calhoun. Pete wanted out. Mr. Peter Calhoun, Jr. began to become scared of being married. He told me that his own father and mother didn't get along. Mr. Peter Calhoun, Sr. was an alcoholic. Fights often turned violent when the children were younger, now his grown children held him back. Mattie, age 32, Mae, age 26 and Peter, Jr., age 29; and Evelyn, usually made Peter, Sr. calm down, but it turned out to be a weekly thing.

There were times when my husband was terrific. I called him, "Fathead," and he named me "Foxx or 47." Foxx because I was pretty and a foxy dresser; and 47 for the year I was born. That was the condition of things the year I told him about a scholarship to attend Wharton School of Business, University of Pennsylvania, when I discovered a book titled, "101 Scholarships for Blacks and Minorities." He won a scholarship and worked towards an MBA in Accounting.

Whenever pressure hit him – he changed dramatically, blaming everybody but himself for everything, including his lack of success, happiness and money. My mother still supplied us with food. His mother still gave him money, perhaps to control him. Pete had long ago replaced her husband and was the man of his mother's household. Their joy seemed to be having weekend card parties and laughing and fighting over the games.

Often, I'd crawl into bed and go to sleep while they were downstairs at Mattie's house. Most times, I'd awake to cursing and loud noises. That meant that Pete was losing and drops of sweat would bead on his forehead. The players would get his silent treatment. If he won, he was loud, smiling, and joking.

"There you go! A Boston! You get the picture," Pete yelled, slapping his cards against the table.

Then back at home one night, Peter said, "The Wharton teachers are prejudiced. One of them had the nerve to ask me" what you smoking in that pipe?"

Funny thing is, I remember Pete adding something to the tobacco in his pipe, which the teacher could possibly smell. While Peter was in school, I kept my job at OIC and worked as his secretary on the side, so I needed my rest. I also attended school for Accounting at Temple University. That was Pete's idea. I hated accounting.

After working my regular job of typing long tax forms and loan applications, I also typed schedules of accounting income statements and balance sheets. Those ten years of small business was a daily routine for me. I even secured clients for my husband's business (SBA loan applicants). I'd work all night and my body had become so exhausted, it seemed I had become the machine and Lorine, the person did not exist anymore.

There was only one good side to being married. For the first time, I had a name and an identity. I was Mrs. Lorine W. Calhoun. I got used to hearing my own first name and a different last name, though a few people still called me "Twin." I loved hearing my own name and feeling the power of my own identity.

I am proud to say that Lorise moved on, out of my shadow of being "the married, successful twin." She decided to attend college, the University of Rhode Island. A minister affiliated with OIC had 100 scholarships aimed at educating needy Black children. Upon hearing the story of our family, 11 children and none were college-educated, he and his committee gave one of those scholarships to Lorise. I was already married and couldn't be considered.

We were at a crossroads in our lives. Yes, I wanted to attend college with her, but my path was to be different. She still worked at OIC when she drove home to Philly from the University on weekends and holidays. She was the first in the family to attend college full-time. A jealous sister-in-law had said, "Lorise is going to a farming school in Rhode Island."

I believe now is an appropriate time to mention a thought that I feel strongly about, and it is this: When a man proposes to you, make darn sure the ring is paid for. Make sure his family is not evil, jealous, or culturally deprived – like just living to gossip with each other about other people because they have no education to create a conversation about anything else in the secular world. When they're so envious of your progress, they can make up lies about you and try to spread them around town to make other people dislike you – you'd better pay attention and stay clear of that love. Don't spend your money paying for your own engagement ring. Even if you can't afford the ring – he cannot afford you.

Listen to me! I didn't mind helping to pay for our dining room set or bedroom set. It took me three years to pay for the 3/4 karat diamond ring and two extra years to pay for the bedroom set. I, on the other hand, was so desperate for a successful marriage and achievements in life, I was willing to work hard for it. I knew I could make Pete into a great husband, even though it was clear that Pete didn't want to grow up. He seemed scared that if I quit work, he would not be able to handle caring for me, let alone a child.

In 1970 I got pregnant and Pete rewarded me with a hard punch in my eye. He walked off, sat at the kitchen table and threw back a scotch. I couldn't believe it, the first time in a four-year marriage.

"What did you go and do that for?" I cried for three days straight. It seemed he was an alcoholic because he drank weekly. Was he a wife beater too? I just could not believe it; no, not my husband. It all happened so unexpectedly, so fast. I kept trying to figure out what I did that was so terrible. I reeled backward and saw flashes of light, red, blue, and green strings of light. I had tried to fight back, landing a couple of punches, but he was 175 pounds to my 105 pounds. He hit me again. I ran with all my might. What set him off? I will never know. That's why I chose to run and I ran with all my might.

I felt ashamed and not sure if I was seriously hurt. I ran around the corner to a house that had a vacant vestibule. So, I crawled up on the cement floor, curled up and let out a long, hard cry. When I was cried out – I thought about Pete, who was now drinking and using dope, also. The cold hardness of the cement floor ran through my whole body. About an hour later, I calmed down and thought Pete had cooled off, too. I got up and walked towards home, facing the dark, unknown shadows. I returned home, not knowing what to expect. I was relieved when he didn't try to hit me again. Instead, we made up, and the next day he brought me beautiful red roses like the color of blood from my lips.

"I am so sorry," Pete begged, "it'll never happen again."

I didn't have sense enough to ask him why he hit me. Why? Why didn't I have a reason or sufficient self-esteem enough to ask him? I guess I was just too wary of taking the chance of upsetting him again. I needed the cuddling he could give. I needed his approval. I needed his whispers. I needed his ugly, undependable angry love. Emotions were heightening and I became totally blind, stupid, and deaf. Love still kept me from seeing the real Pete. When that 1965 jet blue Corvair convertible came to my door and he had liquor, I should have put that man out of my life.

Pete taught me to drive his car, a standard, and things were alright since I did most of the driving. Another clear-cut sign was at the wedding when the groomsmen and Pete smelled of alcohol; I should have run away, I told myself. At this point, my mother had questions and wondered about her pregnant daughter and the survival of her marriage. Things started moving faster. I was in a car accident when I was four months pregnant. While going to work, a truck hit my car. I was in the fast third lane and a truck rear-ended my car. I was distraught that my child's health was in danger. I wanted to make sure everything was alright with my pregnancy, so I was admitted to Westside Park Hospital. I was afraid and in pain. The cold, white room reminded me of the time the gynecologist rammed his fingers inside my body with my legs spread apart.

"You need rest," the doctor and nurses said.

After many tests, one of the results showed that I had a stye on my left eye. I would have to see through that for the rest of my life, but it didn't endanger my vision. Because I was pregnant, the doctor gave me very little medication. For four nights, the older patients cried and moaned all night long and I could hardly sleep. I wanted out.

A beautiful young woman, my hospital roommate, tried to console me. "You should name your child Patrice."

Well, that doesn't remind me of a boy's name, I thought – and my intuition told me it was a boy – a baby boy because, in those days, the baby's sex was anybody's guess. In Pete's family, there was a Mattie and Mae, both Pete's sisters had "M" names and an "M" name would honor the Calhoun Family. My husband and I made a pact that our kids would be named after us, the parents.

"I'll think about it", I said to my roomie, "Patrice has a nice ring to it and Patrice rhymes with Lorise, my twin sister's name."

I didn't want to hurt her feelings, as she was kind. *Please, GOD, get me out of here; I am getting sicker and sicker right here in this hospital! I can't rest.*

A Pact With God

Finally, the doctors let me go home. Life promised to get better and I believed it would.

Lorine W. Calhoun

CHAPTER 18
Birth of First Child

Childbirth is a life-changing situation, no matter in what circumstances you live ~

In the summer of 1971, I felt that being pregnant would be fine if it hadn't been so hot. The daughter of my girl friend and neighbor, Charlotte, would not come near me for some reason. According to an old wives' tale, this meant I was having a girl. I'd see about that.

I was learning to make ceramics at the Naval Base Hobby Shop located in South Philadelphia and also went for checkups at the Philadelphia Naval Hospital, a half-mile away. Meanwhile, Charlotte, who liked to smoke pot with my husband, traveled the 45-minute ride with me to the naval base. I was teaching myself not to judge her bad-girl habit of smoking pot and a few other moral deficits because she would go with me anywhere at a moment's notice. She laughed a lot, which made me feel human. I figured out that Charlotte was a hippie and allowed her in my life only because I really couldn't do anything about it. Pete liked her company, too.

On July 29, 1971, my first labor pains hit. Those were not the little false labor pains from the last week. When my water broke in the bathroom, Pete was nowhere to be found. I screamed, prayed, and marched around the tiny space until Pete came home around 4:30 that afternoon. He grabbed my arm and helped me to the car and we sped on the express-way. It was stop-and-go traffic. Five o'clock became 6:00 o'clock and the pains started coming harder and closer together. I cried and yelled each time a pain hit – 15 minutes apart, then 10 minutes apart and soon there were only 5 minutes between what felt like death blows.

"Oh! My God. Oh! My God. How far is the hospital?" I yelled.

Pete weaved in and out of traffic and after we survived skids and weaving between cars and trucks, he stopped and rushed me into the hospital. Nurses rushed me inside but made me wait a long time to make sure the pains were not false labor. An hour later, Pete was right there in the labor room, telling me how to have this child, directing me to breathe.

"Hold on!" he yelled.

"Shut up, you no good dog! You got me in this mess," I screamed, hitting the air as if it were him.

"I'll leave," Pete said.

"No, don't go!" Sweat dripped from my forehead and pain pierced every cell in my being. The doctors gave me Demerol, but the pain got worse.

"Breathe like a dog," Pete said. "Huh, huh, huh." Now hold on and be patient and wait for the next pain." He kept directing and telling me what to do, blowing through his mouth. He demonstrated, but I didn't want anyone telling me what to do, least of all, Pete. I had a mixture of rage and hate; love and near forgiveness. Mostly, I wanted to kill my husband, but the pain just would not allow me. He was the one who put me through this pain and now he had the nerve to be standing at my bedside. But maybe he really loved me. Maybe I still loved him. I was scared and nervous. How dare Pete!

"SHUT UP!" I yelled.

"I'm leaving for sure this time," I grabbed his arm and Pete knew not to move another inch. He tried to be quiet and obey my wishes, but being the type of person he was, a know-it-all, he kept telling me what to do! Pete wiped his sweat and mine. Bending over me and holding my tear-wet hand, he tried to block my crying sounds.

"Keep pushing, keep pushing," the doctor said.

I cursed everyone I could think of. A monumental pain hit again. Then finally, a death-kind of pain stabbed me. It was an unbearable attack.

"Keep pushing," the doctor urged.

The whole world was coming to an end when Lorine Monica Patrice Calhoun slid from my body like wet soap. It was July 29, 1971. The round-faced clock on the wall read 7:30 in the evening when my beautiful 5-pound, two-ounce baby girl eased into this cruel but often wonderful world. My pretty baby occupied the hurt, bruised, wounded, beaten part of my life in her tiny but strong, gripping hands. I will see to it that she makes something special out of her life. I will!

CHAPTER 19

Second Generation of Love and Hate

Hate burns in your soul and only love can replace it.

My child's well-being stirred in my brain, in my soul, in my cells. It was the center of all my movements.

I didn't want to leave Monica unattended. I tried to be responsible for her every move and her joy. Suddenly, happiness came over me. However, that happiness soon turned into sadness when anxiety made me realize that I had to grow up fast! I must have been suffering from post-partum depression and at the same time, Lorise called me crying.

She was crying into the telephone because a stalker was on campus and he was appearing and disappearing in the shadows everywhere she went. I was crying from post-partum depression and I cried for her too.

Although we were hundreds of miles apart, Lorise at the University of Rhode Island and I in Philadelphia, we still had our unstoppable identical twin connection.

"I felt all of your labor pains," Lorise cried. "It was terrible."

"Why don't they put him out of the University?" I asked. "I don't know."

We both continued to cry.

"Just hold on Lorise. You know how important it is for you and me to get an education in this family. You're the first full-time college student in our family."

Then our crying became louder. I thought we were crying for a better world, crying because we had to grow up, perhaps without leaning on each other as much as we did in the past. We cried until we knew the telephone bill would have to be paid soon.

My mind drifted to the time before Monica came into the world and all that had happened. In the days and weeks prior, things got worse in my marriage, if that was possible. As Pete was finishing his studies at Wharton University, he had started adding pot to the tobacco in his pipe. He began to talk down to me, making me feel smaller than an ant.

As soon as he graduated from Wharton School, Pete added the low-life habit of trying to sell drugs even after I supported him through graduate school and the opening of his own business. I wasn't taking it anymore. I went straight to his mother's house and stood in her face.

"Mrs. Calhoun, did you know your son is selling drugs?" "No, no, not Pete. Are you crazy?"

I rushed out of her house and the next thing I heard was that she marched down to Wharton and questioned one of his friends about Pete selling drugs. His friend got so afraid of that woman flashing her pistol that he told the truth. Then she turned from Pete's friend to Pete.

"I'd better not ever hear of you trying to sell drugs again. You hear me? Cause if I do, I'm going to the dean's office and I'm gonna tell him and you sure will get your license snatched from you. Moreover, if I ever hear of you hittin' my daughter-in-law again, I'm coming at you with my gun and the police."

Peter had kept to himself for about four months until Lorine Monica Patrice was born. Her life made me so happy that I almost forgot who Peter was. He didn't really exist anymore until that day he balled his fist and threw that punch straight at my face. It landed right in my baby's little face as she nursed on my breast. She screamed. I ran under the hanging clothes in the closet. The following day, Monica's face was swollen and her little eye turned black. I read *The Bible* every day, seeking answers while Peter was callous and silent.

One day I was praying and crying when Pete left the house. I then wrapped my baby in a little dingy pink blanket, walked out of the house and drove to a downtown hotel. I made my baby comfortable and lay her on the double-sized bed. I sat beside her, stroking her little face. I dialed Evelyn Calhoun, Pete's mother. I knew she loved the baby and perhaps would guide me to safety.

"You bring that baby back," she said.

"I thought you told me before I married your son that he would never lay a hand on me. Do I have to kill him before you understand?" I cried, shaking, and trembling.

I knew I was growing bolder and bolder while I was on the run with my baby and her swollen face. I sat there for a long time, thinking, waiting to hear from GOD. My mother would be so worried and feeling so guilty, I thought. My brothers might commit murder and go to jail. If I killed him with the butcher knife, I'd probably go to jail and have to leave my baby. My baby was only five-months-old and who would take care of her? Lorise was in college and I wanted that so much for her. I swallowed my good judgment and my pride, lay down and went to sleep with Monica in my arms.

"God, if you allow me, I'll give my marriage one more try! Just look out for my daughter and I'll always honor you as God of my life." I got up and rode home. My mother-in- law was already there. She took my baby and left without a word. I found out the next morning that she went to her sister's home in Baltimore, Maryland. Now Pete, his sisters and his mother's sister stood firmly and united against me. They all said Monica couldn't come back to me because I was unstable. Why did I think she was just bringing me a little relief? I went crazy. My body felt weak and the neighbor found me sitting on the floor in a closet shivering. She took me to the Navy Hospital.

The doctors said, "There's nothing wrong with you. You just need your child back!"

When I got back home, I got on the phone and called my mother-in-law.

"I'll give you one last decent opportunity to bring Monica back to me before I report my child missing and kidnapped. I'll press criminal charges and nobody can stop me. Even death can't stop me."

"I'll bring her back," his mother said.

Four days later, Pete's mother brought Monica back to me.

I felt happy for the first time in months. I realized that I needed to strengthen my backbone and stop playing the victim. I laid down the law that Pete's family couldn't be in our business anymore. Sure, I felt stupid for returning after he hit my child, but I was no longer afraid. I was prepared to die. I didn't know what else to do, but I would do something.

That afternoon his sister blocked my phone calls to our office. That had to stop. When I talked to him that night, I made myself clear.

"First, your sister has to find another job. We are no longer paying her to be your assistant."

I thought of what else I needed to tell him. "Second, your sister Mattie and your mother Evelyn can have no place in our business."

I had just found out that they had purchased land in their names using the money I received from my car accident when I was pregnant. Next, the drugs had to stop, as did his alcohol consumption.

Pete seemed relieved that I had laid down our rules. Things went alright until Pete wanted another child. I was sneaking and taking birth control pills because I was so afraid to get pregnant again, but one morning when I was still tired and sleepy, he caught me. I was so frightened of the violence my first child had brought out in Pete that I had started to have nightmares about it.

"Will you stop hitting me if I have another baby?" I asked, feeling stupid for being such a coward. I had no idea where that kind of humiliation came from and I didn't know where it was going.

"Have one and see," he responded.

How could I allow him to think so little of me? My body and self-respect didn't exist for him nor were my feelings, my life, or my child. Yes, I always tried to keep from getting pregnant. But I was so willing for him to bribe me into visiting the Virgin Islands for a week's vacation with him. The next month, I knew it had happened. Friends suggested that I get an abortion. Pete seemed to be getting crazier by the day.

"I been to the mountain top and talked with God." In the Virgin Islands, there was indeed a beautiful mountain called 'Crown Mountain,' but I doubt if Pete went there and talked with God.

"He needs help and so do you," one friend said. While I was in St. Thomas, I met someone named Eric Burton. He was handsome and kind, a West Indian man from Antigua. You see, when in trouble, we all need someone or something to hold on to. Even if this dream of a man was not real, we still hang on for our lives and stake our hopes and dreams on anything to give us the strength to keep on living. Eric was that angel for me. I have never talked with him since, but he was an illusion and a reason to live, my angel.

Back in Philadelphia, I tried getting an abortion. I went to my local health center and climbed on the table.

"If you had come here and told me that your boyfriend knocked you up and you didn't want your husband to know, we would have given you an abortion, but this would be illegal."

I was scared and very confused, being eight weeks pregnant. Oh no, I could barely walk into the doctor's office for an abortion; now I could barely walk out of it. So, I grabbed my stomach and started crying from my broken heart. Then I screamed inside to the bottom of my rattled soul.

"Your husband is an accountant. The National Society of Public Accountants might sue us; we can't help you!"

That was a landmark learning moment for me. This marked the beginning of my lying career because I suddenly realized I needed to lie to survive in this cold, cruel world of motherhood. Here I was, pregnant and trying to go to school. My employer at OIC, Ms. Anita Chappell, had secured me a scholarship to the Charles Morris Price School of Advertising and Journalism because of the potential she saw in me. Now, what would they say to her about me?

She's trying to improve herself by attending the Charles Moris Price School for Advertising and Journalism, and her husband is having a mental meltdown. I knew that drugs plus alcohol always meant Pete would beat me. Pete was just like his father, Peter Calhoun, Sr., a second-generation alcoholic and a second-generation wife beater.

A psychic once told me I was living with four people: my identical twin sister, me, Peter, and his twin of an alcoholic, wife-beating father. I was living with all those different people. How was it possible to beat all of them? But I had to somehow.

CHAPTER20
Leaving

Everything has its seasons. Some seasons mean one should move on.

Y ou should move out if he's beating on you like you say he is. No court in the world will fault you for moving out."

Those words were a realization, a sign from God to move on. So, I planned to leave on September 12, 1973. We had sex the night before, so Pete wouldn't suspect anything. This final sexual experience sealed the end of a six-year marriage. I was afraid of him, afraid of being pregnant and being beaten again. So, I gave myself willingly to that brute with tears in my eyes.

The next morning Pete left for work at about 8:00o'clock and I was on the phone asking my brother to help me move out a few minutes later.

"Call Cohen, Jr. He has a truck," Bert said.

When Cohen arrived, he beckoned a stranger walking down the street to help. They pushed the floor model RCA Color television set into a pick-up truck. My 1971 Vega was finally packed to the brim. I said goodbye to 532 W. Penn Street, German Town. I muttered my final goodbyes to the brainwashing isolation, violence and the poverty of being materially rich and money poor and to coming home to no heat or electricity in the house.

I had made several attempts at getting help before finally making this move to leave. I desperately wanted the Navy to reopen Pete's file and treat him for mental illness or alcoholism. I tried talking to the Navy and my minister, Dr. Harrison J. Trapp, but they didn't take one step toward helping to fix my marriage or Pete's problems.

Finally, I had tried a marriage counselor. Monica and I sat there as the counselor interviewed Pete on the telephone.

"This is Peter Calhoun, Jr., a graduate from Wharton School, University of Pennsylvania."

Counselor: "Oh, Mr. Calhoun, I am here with your wife and child."

Pete continued, "Where did you graduate from, and what are your credentials for counseling my family or me?"

Counselor: "I went to Penn State and I have a Bachelor's Degree in…"

Pete: "That's not good enough."

Counselor: "If you refuse to come in for a talk, I cannot help you!"

"I wouldn't think of it," Pete said, and I heard the phone click and disconnect.

I left crying. Maybe I wasn't going to win. In the following days, Momma cried out her concern that I would have bad health as I age because of the beatings. Pete tried his sick mind games on Momma just as he had brainwashed me.

"Get out with Monica while you still can," Momma warned me.

"I found my wife in an alley. You know, she could never survive in this world without me." Pete set out to use my mother as his personal psychiatrist and told her all the gory details of each fight and the beatings he gave me. Nevertheless, my mother held my six brothers back from killing my husband, which gave Pete permission to continue beating me. I desperately wanted to leave before it came down to kill or be killed. There were rifles and guns in the house. I knew where they were stashed.

So here was I. It had to come to this. I left. I got married on September 16, 1967, and left him on September 12, 1973. Being pregnant again gave me the strength to leave my husband. After the sixth beating – I was history because Pete beat me in the stomach and I feared for my unborn child. I could still hear his degradation.

"Will you hit me again?" I remembered asking him before I was pregnant.

"Have a child and see," he had said.

The safety of my children became my top priority. Their security was more important than my own. When I tried to leave before, Pete would grab Monica.

"You can go, but not Monica."

So, this time, I waited until he went to work, and by noon I had moved out. I was embarrassed and disgraced, but I moved back home with my mother. My mother had prepared for me to come back home after Pete told her about the beatings.

"If a man hits you once, no matter what he says, he'll hit you again," she said to me.

That day, when Momma came home, I was already settled in. I could tell that Monica was happier already and I felt that her well-being justified my decision. Even at age two, she seemed fearful of our fights. I used to dream that I hated living with my Momma after I married. I had nightmares about living with Pete, throwing chairs, slamming things and slapping me for no reason. Just thinking that I glanced at him the wrong way could spark a beating.

Pete coming home and finding me gone must have sent him into a wild rage of phone calls. After all, who would type all those tax forms and help with his business? Since he didn't show up for a few days, I knew he was just careful not to come by the house as my six brothers would be waiting for him. He was probably scared he couldn't beat them all as he had beat me. That's the thing about wife-beaters; they know who to abuse. He was especially careful of my baby brother Hubert because he was not buying anything Pete was selling and since he was the only one living with Momma then and responsible for the house, he would most likely be home.

In all fairness to my mother, she treated me better than ever. Had I known she would treat me so decently, I would have left Pete a long time ago. I stayed with Momma, but the fights never stopped. My mother-in-law, sisters-in-law and husband kept adding their two cents to everything I said and did – especially about how I was raising Monica.

"You all are fighting over my child like a dog fighting over a piece of meat."

Finally, on March 21, 1974, my labor pains began. My brother, Hubert, dropped me off at the Navy Hospital and left me to fend for myself while he went to work. It hurt that Hubert did that, but it must have been in preparation for me learning to fend for myself. Anyhow, Peter Eric Calhoun, III, was born at five pounds three ounces. The nurse brought him and laid him on my chest.

The nurse said, "He was singing."

"Give me Stevie Wonder or Ray Charles." I noticed he was indeed humming.

I wondered how it would be to have my baby in Momma's home. The days before I left, Pete kept creeping up in my brain. I thought particularly of one incident. Pete rented the television set and wanted to watch sports and I wanted to see movies. We fought over the T.V. We fought about my son's name, too. Earlier, we agreed to name both children after the parents and us. Therefore, I was willing to call my son Pete. Everyone thought I was crazy. But I knew I always endeavored to do the right thing, which is not always the most popular thing to do.

"We will name him Peter David," Pete said.

I no longer lived with Pete and had no plans of ever going back to him. "I'll name him Peter Eric Calhoun, III." After all, I was the one who carried him for nine months. I wanted him named "Eric" after the friend I had met in the Virgin Islands.

The Navy said, "They wouldn't side with either parent."

So, the Navy didn't write a middle name on the birth certificate. My brother Zeke came to visit me and I left the hospital with him. When Pete went to the hospital the next day, he tried to tear down the Philadelphia Naval Hospital because his wife and child were nowhere to be found.

Meanwhile, my new life "began." My mother never allowed any child of hers to be on welfare, but then she told me to get county aid. For seven months, I was on welfare. So, when I told my social worker that I wanted my child to be named Eric, he mailed in a corrected birth certificate and I got the name I wanted for my son, Peter Eric Calhoun, III. I felt it was a reward from GOD for doing the right thing. Now I prayed for more courage to continue my new life. I needed this courage to get out of an abusive marriage and not go back; as well as to stay strong and build a new life for my children and me.

"God, give me a new life and I will become who you want me to be," My pact with God continued. I knew that being a "caring, good mother" was a part of that promise. I knew that my children's lives were bigger than mine. These children were going to have a mother, even if they didn't have a father. Slave stories had taught me that much.

CHAPTER 21

Son in Crisis

In life, when you find your heart, never lose it again.

Something was wrong with Eric. His eyes looked crossed and one eye was bigger than the other. One eye was blue while the other one looked brown and white. His foot slanted to the right and it looked stiff. His doctor put the leg in a cast for six weeks. I ordered corrective shoes. He didn't smile or laugh. Secretly, I wanted no part of him. I trained myself to be happy. If I were happy, then my children would be happy. I made myself breast-feed him for the first six weeks.

At the six-week check-up, the pediatrician scratched his head and called in two outside doctors. After five hours of tests, the doctor referred me to an outside expert. My worst fears took over and I was worried about the time Pete had beaten me in my stomach when Eric was in the womb. My son had been damaged. Now I was being beaten up by raw emotions of something the doctors couldn't diagnose – and something I couldn't bring myself to tell them. During the next two week's spiritual rustlings, I knew deep inside that Eric was blind.

"How did you know?" the doctor asked when I went for the next two-week checkup.

"Number one, Eric has never smiled at me. Number two, every nurse that held him said he was humming as if he needed to entertain himself because he couldn't see anything."

"Your son is blind and nothing can be done for him," Dr. Spann from the Wills Eye Institute said.

I wasn't willing to take his diagnosis as a final answer. Other children in the same hospital were getting eye transplants in one eye and could see afterward. I felt like dying right there on the spot. I wanted to yell out to God and tell Him how betrayed I felt. I wanted to hurl myself from the top story window. I couldn't even recall which floor we were on. My body, brain, nerves and muscles boiled like hot lava. I felt it spewing up and shooting through my veins, but even a volcano was better off than I was because I had no power to release that bubbling internal explosion. God stroked me and I spoke.

"If I bear the pain, disappointment and fear I have gone through, then I can raise my child. Just give me my baby," I said, reaching over and laying him on my chest. Now it was Monica, Eric and me against the world. God would have to be responsible to help raise my children. God had given me a yard-stick in that Monica, my daughter, was born first. I would raise my blind child precisely as I would raise Monica. My mother thought I should raise him as a blind child, but I would raise him with only a few of the hindrances of blind children. I knew that would be a lifetime assignment.

First, I taught myself not to trust anyone with my money since my husband took my $6,000 and bought a house in his name only. I wouldn't make that mistake again. Secondly, GOD taught me how to react to children and adults who asked about Eric's eyes. I taught myself to stop crying after people would ask me about Eric's eyes. I would answer in a way to help them understand and stop being stupid and insensitive.

"His eyes just don't work. Just as we are born Black or white, he was born with eyes that don't work."

Finally, GOD directed me to find and get an appointment with Dr. Harold G. Scheie at the Presbyterian-University of Pennsylvania Medical Center. I was sent there after Judge Charles Wright, Support Court Judge, refused to believe that Eric was blind.

Dr. Scheie wrote back to the Judge: "Eric Calhoun has such profound congenital anomalies that no treatment is in order. In fact, any operation would only lead to the loss of an eye." Dr. Scheie owned his own hospital that was part of the University of Pennsylvania. Everything in the hospital was shaped like an eye. After carefully examining Eric, this kind of elderly gentleman with curly white hair said, "If he was my child, I would not let anyone touch him."

That was that. I trusted that man, that is, until I got a call from Dr. George Calhoun, a doctor from Wills Eye Hospital in North Philadelphia. Well, I was through with the name Calhoun. I hated the husband, the man and the name. So, Dr. Calhoun was meeting me with cards stacked against him because of his name. But, he had all the new machinery my son might need to get his eyes fixed. Dr. Calhoun wasn't a big talker.

"I want to operate on Eric Monday after Father's Day."

A Pact With God

When my family heard the news, they pitched a fit. They didn't trust any experimental operation on Eric. No one trusted any white doctor experimenting on Black babies back then and neither did I. I didn't trust him with my baby. So that was that.

Next, I got news of new machinery at the U.S. Navy Hospital. They could send me to New Orleans, where they could perform a new test on Eric. Word soon came back from the U.S. Navy that The Wills Eye Clinic had the same machinery in Philadelphia. The Navy would not send me anywhere to get an expert opinion. So, I decided to take my child to New York for the third opinion. I placed Eric in a car bed in the back seat of my lime green 1971 Vega and drove to New York and knocked on some doors.

Presbyterian Hospital and the Brooklyn Eye and Ear Hospital were the first try. By the time I had walked stairs in high rises and put my shoes on and then off, none of the doctors wanted any part of Eric and me. I remembered what Dr. Scheie had said about not letting anyone touch him. I also remembered what Dr. Calhoun said, "I want to get in there and see if I can save something, even a retina."

At last, I think I was beginning to trust Dr. Calhoun. I was starting to feel like Mary in *The Bible*. There was no room in the Inn for my child and me. But I wouldn't stop. I drove to Mount Sinai Hospital and met a man who answered to the name of Dr. Zinn.

"I can examine Eric, and he would be placed under anesthesia on the Monday after Father's Day."

That was the same day Dr. Calhoun wanted to operate on Eric. Was this a sign from heaven? My aunt, Eddie Mae, who had breast cancer, welcomed Eric and me into her home. We both tried to rest but couldn't. Eric could not be fed for 24 hours before going under anesthesia. So, he cried all night long.

At the same time, my mother called. "Lorine, Pete stole Monica from the babysitter."

My mind raced through a hundred horror scenes where mentally ill Pete might try to torture my daughter. I died inside, I cried inside, and I cried silently to myself. But that night, Eric and I just cried together.

By seven o'clock in the morning, Dr. Zinn finished his interview with me and wasted no time shaking his head. I fell in and out of sleep in a chair inside the waiting room while Eric went through the tests. Finally, they woke me up. The doctor stood there patiently while I got my senses together. Then he spoke to me slowly and kindly.

"According to our tests, Eric doesn't even see light. The retinas are detached, but the pressure is good. Still, no operation is going to correct Eric's eye problems. If Dr. Calhoun had operated, he wouldn't have done anything good or right."

I didn't say a word. I couldn't say a word. I tried to imagine Eric's stroke of misfortune reaching into the recovery room before taking the ride back home. Eric and I made the two-and-a-half-hour drive back to Philadelphia in silence. My heart would barely stay inside of me. I eyed the road and Eric at the same time. It had been hours since he and I really slept. We just stared out into the darkness together. I could still hear the doctor's prognosis.

"We had to give him double the anesthetic because the little fellow is so strong."

Little did I know that I would forever have to depend on Eric's strength for the rest of my life.

I stopped by my old house, 232 West Penn Street in German town, Pa. and called the police. I used my key to the house and found Monica, my daughter licking sugar from a spoon like a horse. I picked her up and wiped her mouth and held her close to me. When the police came, I told the police that my husband was mentally ill and had a gun. Pete peeked his head out the door.

"Not the police again. Where do you think you're going?"

I threw Monica on my hip and ran to the car with both children and drove to my mother's house. That's what a woman does when she's lost every bit of herself. I went back to a place that had betrayed me in many ways before. I said it was because my Momma didn't know any better and surely, I didn't either.

As soon as I got in the door, the phone rang and I answered with nothing but stress in my voice. The voice on the other end of the phone was Dr. Calhoun.

"Why didn't you let me operate on, Eric?" asked Dr. Calhoun.

"I drove to New York and Dr. Zinn at Mount Sinai Hospital told me he doubted if you would have done anything good or right," I responded.

"What are you talking about? I'm ordering the tests done at Dr. Zinn's office so I can see for myself."

The zombie in me didn't answer. The following morning,

Lorine W. Calhoun

I woke up to Dr. Calhoun's call.

"He was right. If I had operated, I doubt if I would have been able to help Eric at all. Eric doesn't even see light."

My heart sank, but my resolve stood up. I was going to live. I was going to raise my two children. I had the supernatural lens to see the future. I didn't always turn to it, or use it, but now I did have it and I was going to make something of myself and my children. One day soon, I was going to see it and do it all. Then I would know what joy feels like again.

CHAPTER 22

The Move

Moving up in life is courageous.

I landed at my mother's house in the middle of the night and swore I never wanted to see Pete Calhoun again. At the same minute, I heard the doorbell ring.

"Lemme see Monica," Pete said, still banging on the door and ringing the doorbell at the same time.

Hubert yelled back. "You gonna bring a woman with you to pick up your daughter?"

A long pause hung between outside and inside. The sound of a car speeding off shook the porch. In a half-hour, Peter was banging on the door again. It was Mae, Pete's sister.

"You're wrong, Hubie. She was me the whole time," she said.

Hubert grabbed the gun and stood guard over the front door. Pete kept on knocking.

"Monica! Monica!" Those same words in between crying and knocking.

About midnight, the door was still in place, and Hubert

walked away and hid the gun in the drawer. I knew someone was going to get hurt and I didn't want the blood of my children's father on my hands. I remembered how quickly brutal things could happen. I didn't want my baby brother to face prison because of my mistake of marrying a crazy alcoholic.

Just a year before, the police officers jumped on my husband's side after walking into our beautiful home and seeing the black slate rock and wood furniture, red tapestry couch and rocking chair and hardwood floors. There was a pecan brown bedroom set and our open dining room, along with a spacious kitchen area. This was used to determine the verdict in the case of whether Peter Calhoun was guilty. They said Peter did nothing wrong, even though I had scars.

So now, the police knocked on my door and identified himself; and I asked what he wanted as Hubert opened the door.

"Madam, I am Officer Clark, is this your husband?" "Yes, sir."

Pete looked tired and at a loss for words. His head was down but I had seen fear darted about in his eyes.

"Peter Calhoun, Jr., you were caught on an airplane with a gun. The plane was vacant."

"I was doing a feasibility study," Pete said.

"You need to come with us," one of the officers said. I called his mother for advice.
"Don't let them take him," Mrs. Calhoun cried. "We're

taking him downtown," Officer Clark said. "No, not my son.

Don't let them take him, Lorine."

A Pact With God

My mother decided that after he paraded me around to show other family members how he had to beat me up to make me behave, she told the cops to take him. I thought of my blind child and the possibility that his father might act foolishly and get shot by the police. I told myself that I didn't want his blood on my hands. I told the police that he was on medication and I would see that he took it. Then I prayed that God would help me make a better decision; to be stronger than him so that I would never be subject to another madman.

Lorine W. Calhoun

CHAPTER 23

Trip to Miami, Fla. and St. Thomas, Virgin Islands

I had faith. So, God needed to guide my path into the Virgin Islands.

Before getting to the Virgin Islands, we had to get to Miami. Cohen Jr., my oldest nephew, didn't like my husband, and once again, he stepped up to the plate when I asked him to drive me to Miami. He had helped me move from Penn Street to my mother's home just eleven months earlier. Out of sixteen nieces and nephews in the Willis Family, Cohen Jr. was the only one willing to help me relocate to the Virgin Islands. The older children had an unspoken duty to set a good example for the younger sixteen nieces and nephews. It was that generation that we prayed would break the cycle of the men being sold off or broken away from the family. They were to show victory over that monster that had gripped and damaged the average Black family and stole its way right down through the generations. I was proud of him and told him so.

It depressed me that Lorise had finished her four-year degree and was a consultant at a Sears Shopping Center in Albany, New York, because we were separated for long

121

periods of time. Maybe it seemed like I'd never get to finish school. No, I was plain jealous. No, I couldn't be jealous because I was dead set on getting my degree too, and soon.

Lorise's progress tossed my mind about as we burned up the highways charging towards Miami. For some reason, I kept remembering Lorise's condominium in Albany, New York, where I met a blind family living a normal life – a husband, wife and four children. A housekeeper came in to clean, but everything else was done by the blind husband and his blind wife. The children all had eye problems and got operations. I think I cherished that moment and it was etched into my brain.

I wrestled with the fact that I had never been attended to by a Black doctor or was led by Black political figures. We just did not have any Black doctors around and neighborhood Blacks didn't do much work in the political races. However, young Blacks started getting involved in Civil Rights. I believed that's how we would make our lives and communities better. You see, things were happening; we began to feel the crackling energy in our lives. It was in the air. I could feel it.

As the car shook and sped along, I tried to put my life together in my mind. Can I be the captain of my soul? Can I start entirely over in a new country? Can I build something out of the shambles of a bad marriage?

A car honked in the distance and the past seemed to be rolling away behind us. My mother's favorite grandchildren were leaving because my only son was born blind. She would brag on him and spoil him. But life was too hard for him for me to allow her or anyone to spoil him. I silently vowed to raise Eric as a normal, healthy human being. My heart filled and pumped with that "vow". Just before we left Philadelphia, Momma had a spiritualist come to our house and pray for us. The older lady went on talking for a while, then she said, "You have no idea what the Good Lord has in mind for her," she pointed at me. "Be of good cheer. Lean on God. Let her go."

I could see my mother's pain, guilt, regret, and frustration.

"God will only give her what you and she can handle," the spiritualist said. "God Bless you. You are both brave and strong."

I had been glad to hear her positive promises. I began thinking of how my brothers didn't help me move. When it came time for John D., my oldest brother's turn to be remembered, I had to laugh. He was dangerous and half crazy. When he went to visit Lorise at the University of Rhode Island, she had to hide her girlfriends because John D. thought he was every girl's dream and a married man without repentance.

In the middle of that reverie, the truck behind us that was carrying my personal belongings started smoking and snorting and broke down. We jumped out and found that the engine didn't have a drop of oil in it. Given, Cohen Jr. was a mechanic, but he couldn't fix that truck. We left it where it stood and had to send someone back for it. I didn't know if I would see my belongings again. The babies were stirring and crying. I fixed bottles and fed Eric; I gave Monica some apple sauce.

At 7:30 that evening, August 10, 1974, we pulled into Miami after a six-hour drive. The children were tired and sleepy, but the place was beautiful. My dressmaker's mother, who made those aqua blue satin dresses Lorise and I ordered, invited us to spend the night. She was so warm and lovely. She opened a fancy bathroom for the children and me to shower. Then she fed us a full meal and we caught up on the Philly gossip. At 6 o'clock the next morning, I dressed the children and me, said a huge thanks to our gracious host and we were off. We boarded a plane to the Virgin Islands.

I must say thanks to my twin, Lorise who contributed financially to my move. I had gotten money from her as she had gotten from me when she moved to Rhode Island. We are not just sisters; but we support each other too. Thank God, I made it to St. Thomas in time for school. I found that OIC was located in St. Croix and not St. Thomas. Because of that distance, I could only find work at the College.

Due to the challenges I had in travelling from home to Miami, the volunteer truck driver had placed my personal belongings on a Greyhound bus so that they could be transported to St. Thomas. The things were not really that important, as I had the most important things in my life with me, my two children. Now no court or no one could give me grief about them. Heaven seemed to continue to smile on me. Life had taught me that only a mother's faith in God and love could maneuver families through any storm. Right then, I realized I had kidnapped my children. I wondered if the United States government would come and return us all to the United States to end this struggle. My numbness kept me from being afraid, from pain and from thoughts of any consequences. Nothing could be worse than what I had been living.

To all my good Samaritans, thank you for helping me open a new door in my life for all the world to see! I was going to live in St. Thomas and had graduated from the Charles Morris

Price School of Advertising and Journalism with a Certificate in both Advertising and Journalism in 1974. I was going to get another degree.

Spiritually, I could see Los Angeles, California. It was dry but green. There were oranges hanging from trees and Hollywood lay just northwest of the City of Angels. I pondered why I always imagined Hollywood to look so great. The weather was warm in the daytime and the ocean breeze came like a sweet touch that brought the cool nights. I could feel that place and hear it. In the daytime, I could touch it as the sun lay warm against my wounded back. I had taken my first step into fearlessness and I would die rather than go back. I didn't try to consider what was lying ahead of me in St. Thomas, but one thing I knew for sure was my determination to move forward. Although death seemed to be waiting around the corner for my children and me, I felt no pain. I was numb to pain. I was going to become somebody. The following day I had to go to the University to register for school and put together a million pieces that would give me a life in St. Thomas.

I invite you to come with me to my next book, A PACT WITH GOD 2 and see how God has answered my PACT with Him. For now, though, I see a spiritual and fulfilled life in Hollywood, California. Watch me as this unlimited power unfolds. I will share every detail of a young woman with a blind baby in her arms and a three-year-old at her side, all without money and not yet enrolled in school, overcoming problem after problem. I steadily march toward my vision toward my spiritual promises. I know I'm going to make it.

Just wait and see.

Book 2-coming soon!

A PACT WITH GOD – life in Hollywood.

TESTIMONIALS

From MONICA CALHOUN, my daughter:

My mother has shown the determination of a strong Black woman who makes A PACT WITH GOD to raise two unlikely children. Further, she demonstrates many post-slavery Black people's passages from the South to the North, called her "Promised Land." Yet, her woes had just begun. It seems to me, an image that says, "If one woman's courage can make a difference, we all should take that same courage and move forward." She was never afraid; she never shrank in the face of danger.

From ERIC CALHOUN, my son:

As an only son, my mother has been not only a fantastic parent but an awesome friend to my sister Monica Calhoun and me. I love my mother for who she is and for her training and the values she instilled in me. Because of her, I am a totally independent young man. She taught me ways to survive and overcome the dark world where I was born. I enjoy my life much the same as a person with sight because of my mother's love and her relationship with spiritual wonders. I do almost everything that a person with sight does. She gave me self-reliance, and self-reliance makes me feel the world is worth living fully.

atthetopoflife@aol.com (author) & starproductions5341@gmail.com (author)

atthetopproductions.com & greatestlifeforever.com

Made in the USA
Columbia, SC
17 June 2021